BILLIARDS

AS IT SHOULD BE PLAYED

by **WILLIE HOPPE**
(Edited by Byron Schoeman)

Contemporary Books, Inc.
Chicago

Published by Contemporary Books, Inc.
180 North Michigan Avenue, Chicago, Illinois 60601
Manufactured in the United States of America
Library of Congress Catalog Card Number: 78-59585
International Standard Book Number: 0-8092-8837-0 (cloth)
0-8092-7402-7 (paper)

Published simultaneously in Canada by
Beaverbooks
953 Dillingham Road
Pickering, Ontario L1W 1Z7
Canada

AUTHOR'S FOREWORD

I REALIZE how easy it is to confuse the raw beginner in billiards with a dry fusillade of intricate, complicated technical terms, diagrams, and photographs.

My instruction system always has been based on the theory that a sound billiard game is founded on the simple fundamentals and not on any complicated groundwork.

I dwell only on the A B C's of the game—the stance, grip, bridge, stroke, etc., before going into fundamental shots, and rules to follow in order to make them easily.

Even the celebrated 3-cushion "Diamond System" can be mastered if you take each lesson step-by-step and don't eat your dessert before your soup. For the first time in any publication, I have fully explained the "Diamond System" in entirety—with diagrams. But, remember, first learn the fundamentals and basic principles and shots. If you think you know all this already—go over it again. It's like seeing a show twice—you always find something you missed.

Through the explanations, photographs and diagrams in this book, I show you what I know you should know and practice in order to enable you to develop your own game to its greatest possibilities. As you apply these instructions, remember that there is no standard form in any sport—only by experiment will you develop your own distinctive style. Determine your best form as quickly as possible and concentrate on that until you are "in the groove," and then, but not before, begin to think about the balls and your score.

The instruction set forth in this volume is intended not only for those who desire to begin playing after they have grown up, but for those players who have started out on the wrong foot, those others who want to improve their game, as well as for the youngsters.

There is no reason why anyone taking up the game for the first time, or wanting to improve, may not do so with sound hopes of reasonable success. There remains only this to be said on the subject: Do not expect too much in the beginning. Some persons have more athletic aptitude than others, better co-ordination of mind and muscle, and consequently they learn more quickly. But, in any event, a game which has endured from our earliest ages and which now numbers approximately 10,000,000 players in the United States alone must have a definite and lasting appeal.

My best effort has been made to present, in the simplest form, those methods which should be productive of quickest and most satisfactory results in the game of the average billiard player. Fundamentals should be mastered before going ahead with advanced play. Without fundamentals, a player starts with a handicap.

You or anyone else who reads these instructions can become a good billiard player beyond the shadow of a doubt—if you follow them. My sole hope is that I have succeeded in my intention and that this book also will prove a source of enjoyment and assistance to you and everyone who likes to make, and see, ivory trickle over the green baize—the game to which I have devoted my life.

Wishing you every success in the "Game for all,"

Sincerely,

Willie Hoppe

BILLIARDS AS IT SHOULD BE PLAYED

By WILLIE HOPPE

(Edited by Byron Schoeman)

Selection of The Proper Cue

THE cue is one of the most important playing factors. Give a player a cue that he can handle and watch him step. The principal elements to consider in the cue are its weight, length, size and kind of tip, grip, spine, taper (shape), balance, and its general playing qualities. Its upkeep and the proper use of chalk on its tip also are valuable to know.

While these may seem trivial to the average player, they are of an importance easily apparent to an expert or semi-skilled player. The cue's significance is the main reason I start "Billiards As It Should Be Played" with "Selection of the Proper Cue."

WEIGHT OF CUE

Billiard players frequently make the mistake of choosing a very heavy, long cue with a small tip. I urge all players to use an 18 to 20 ounce cue, 54 to 56 inches long, with a tip one-half inch in diameter.

The fact that a very heavy cue enables a player to get greater distance into a cue ball seems to appeal to most players, who like to see a ball hit a lot of cushions. That, of course, is the reason a heavier cue is desirable for 3-cushion play. It is necessary to drive the ball further in 3-cushions than in straight-rail, cushion-caroms, balkline or pocket-billiards.

It is both valuable and interesting to note that all the expert professionals use cues of about the same weight and length. Welker Cochran's is the heaviest cue among the experts, weighing 21 ounces. Jake Schaefer uses a 19 ounce cue. Almost every topflight player of note uses a cue weighing between 19 and 21 ounces. I know of no leading player who uses a cue weighing more than 21 ounces. The average cue weight used by the stars is 20 ounces. I use a cue weighing between $19\frac{1}{2}$ and $19\frac{3}{4}$ ounces.

LENGTH OF CUE

As to length of cue, there is but little variation. The leading players favor cues 54 to 57 inches long. A cue measuring 55 inches is, in the majority of cases, plenty long enough for 3-cushions. I use a 55 inch cue for 3-cushions. For straight-rail, cushion-caroms, balkline, and other styles of play, I advocate a cue 54 inches long.

CUE TIPS

Use tips which measure approximately one-half inch in diameter. Many players, beginners and experienced, prefer a small tip, but it has been proved that accuracy and firmness of stroke and control of the cue ball are better obtained with a one-half inch tip.

Professional players use a very hard leather tip. It is necessary that only the surface be soft enough to permit a slight roughening so that chalk will take hold. Soft tips are to be avoided.

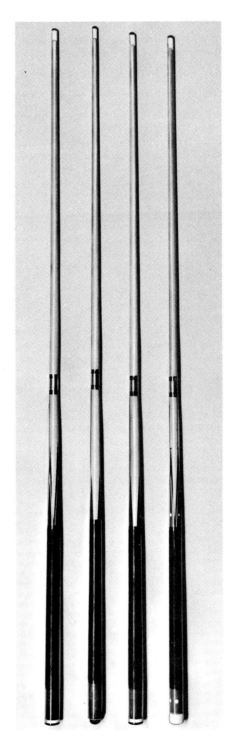

(Photograph No. 1)—Jointed Cues—Hoppe Style. Note four different styles have little variation.

SUITABILITY TO YOU

Select a cue in harmony with your physical powers. Take special care to select the right taper. Some players prefer slender types, others thick models in either shafts, grips or both. I advise all players to own their own cues, preferably jointed ones of my design. (See Photograph No. 1.)

If you do not possess a private cue, become accustomed, as much as possible, to playing with cues of similar weight and length. A cue, if too heavy, will paralyze the nerves of the arm and render them unable to estimate correctly the amount of force employed, which, among other things, greatly affects the all important playing factor, speed. On the other hand, if the cue is too light, it will call for too much force to allow a steady and deliberate aim. Without some sensation communicated to the hand through the cue, when it comes in contact with the cue ball, it would be impossible to play good billiards.

JOINTED CUES — TAPER OF SHAFTS

As previously stated, jointed cues are preferable. A jointed cue is made in two parts—shaft and butt—connected by a screw joint that can easily be taken apart. When shafts become crooked, badly worn, or broken, they then can be replaced. Players who travel from room to room to play their favorite game find a jointed cue a great convenience, too.

All experts use jointed cues with extra shafts. When something goes wrong with one of their shafts, they then can immediately replace it with another. Select the shaft thickness that conforms most comfortably to your bridge hand. (See Photograph No. 1.)

GRIPS

Grips are made of leather, twine, silk, and cork. I recommend and use a leather grip. So do most of the top-flight professionals. The size of the grip—thick or thin—is optional, depending on the individual player's requirements.

HOW TO CARE FOR YOUR CUE

When not in use, a cue should be kept in a cue rack, away from excessive heat or dampness to prevent warping. A cue must be straight, for any crookedness not only distracts the eye, but seriously interferes with playing. If the cue has not sufficient "spine", it bends slightly before actually starting the ball on its course. Not enough to see with the naked eye, but it bends, nevertheless. Result —an erratic shot. (See Diagram No. 1.)

A cue should be well sand-papered occasionally with fine sand-paper. The leather tip, particularly, requires frequent sand-papering to keep it from projecting over the cue. This projection of the leather, which is caused by contact with the ball, often causes miscues. The leather should be kept even with the cue and slightly rounded on the top.

Cue tips are used on the points of cues to absorb all the force of each shot. They must withstand a tremendous amount of abuse and punishment. They also must provide a fine surface with which to stroke the ball, and impart the correct action to the cue ball.

The leather tip, therefore, is most important, on account of direct contact with the ball.

For these reasons, when your cue tip becomes too hard and glossy or too soft, tap the tip with a fine cut file. Tap the top of the cue tip with sharp, glancing blows. File until surface is slightly rough, which will enable tip to take and hold chalk much better. Do not use file in a scraping movement; it will tear your tip.

Then take a damp cloth and wet sides of tip, following with a polishing procedure with back of sandpaper or with a smooth piece of leather. This hardens the sides, insures a firm tip, and prevents tip from spreading.

ALWAYS REMEMBER: A properly trimmed and shaped tip will hold chalk much better, therefore guaranteeing less miscues and, of course, better play.

HOW TO USE CHALK

Chalk provides an abrasive film between the leather of the cue tip and the surface of the cue ball, causing adherence and helping the cue to impart proper action

(Diagram No. 1)—An exaggerated picture of how a spineless cue acts in actual play.

to the ball. Chalk prevents miscues—and miscues are often the difference between good and poor playing—winning or losing a game.

The proper way to chalk a tip is to hold a piece of chalk perfectly horizontal on the top of the tip and revolve the chalk with a few brisk half-motions of the wrist over the tip. Tilt slightly to chalk the edges. Don't revolve the cue tip under a steady hand of chalk. This is the mistake made by most players, especially beginners. And don't hold the chalk in an almost vertical position and twist the cue around. In this manner, the edge of the tip is worn to a point, causing miscues, and chalk does not properly adhere to the tip.

A cue that feels 100% comfortable in your hands; not too long or heavy; not too short or light; a proper watch and use of cue tips, and correct and regular chalking of the cue will guarantee, through less miscues, etc., your objective—better billiards.

FUNDAMENTALS—THE KEYNOTE

BILLIARDS, contrary to the belief of some players, is not a difficult and complex game. In its essence, it is simple. The beginner has only to discover and master the fundamentals of the game to enjoy it from the start. It is true, and a pity it is, that a great majority of novices and many who have made some progress in the game have little idea of what these fundamentals are.

They think in terms of the diamond system, angles, bank shots, masse, force-follow, force-draw, and extreme english. They forget, or overlook, the fact that the important thing is to hit the ball correctly. It's a human weakness, I guess, to try to learn billiards, or any game, for that matter, backwards instead of starting at the beginning. In short, learning to play billiards is easy, but it's like going to school, where the first grade comes before the second, and so on.

My explanations are simple, but thorough, in covering fundamentals. If they are followed carefully, and combined with practice, you will be able, from the start, to enjoy this most fascinating of all indoor games.

If you are a beginner, take each lesson in order, each suggestion step-by-step, and master it before going further. If you are already an experienced player—try to forget what you do and how you play—and start all over.

Suggestions outlined have been obtained not only by years of practical study, general knowledge and experience, but also by continually watching the common faults of the average player.

ALWAYS REMEMBER: You are educated; not the balls, table, cue, etc. Under normal conditions, your shots are just what you make them. If you will concentrate, study and practice, you can, without doubt, become a better than ordinary player.

There are seven important fundamental factors to consider first. When you master them you are on the way toward becoming an expert billiard player. These seven essential fundamental factors are:

    (1)—Position at the table (stance);
    (2)—Grip on the cue (balance point);
    (3)—The bridge;
    (4)—Cueing the ball;
    (5)—The stroke (follow-through);
    (6)—Application of english;
    (7)—Speed and force.

The keynote to good billiards, therefore, comprises these seven most essential points in starting or improving your game. If you will bear in mind these factors, you will make steady progress. I shall take each of them in order and it is my determination to discuss and explain their principal points; and how you should solve them.

If you follow these instructions, which you *must* know and practice, you will develop your game to its greatest possibilities.

I had the luck to have a good teacher in the game, my father. I was only five years old when I first took to the game. Father had a little hotel at Cornwall-on-the-Hudson, New York, and the hotel had a combination billiard and pocket-billiard table. I started on the pocket-billiard game and, with my dad's help, made good progress.

We had frequent visits from traveling salesmen, called drummers in those days. When I was about nine years old, one of these salesmen, new to our town, saw me fooling around the table and patronizingly offered to play me a game. I obliged. He broke the balls and I ran out the game in the very first inning. He racked up his cue.

"What kind of town is this?" he muttered. "I'm better than a green hand at this game, but here the babies beat me."

(Photograph No. 2)—Correct First Position at Table (stance)—Side View.

POSITION AT THE TABLE, OR CORRECT STANCE

POSITION at the table, or stance, is of foremost importance in billiards. It must be natural. It must be solid. You should be comfortable, relaxed in posture, and in position to execute the shot facing you.

And that's just where we start—facing the shot. Distance to stand from table can be determined by first placing cue tip almost on cue ball, cue extended horizontal to table bed, with right hand near butt end of cue and at right hip, and by using good judgment and natural instinct.

Face the shot squarely, your feet a slight distance apart, with left foot forward, to give firmness. The cue is held in both hands at the right side; with the right hand on the upper butt of the cue; left hand grasping cue naturally. My feet are from 18 to 19 inches apart, shoe tip to shoe tip. (See Photograph No. 2.)

Then bend your body forward with head directly over and on a line with the cue, which should be sighted as a hunter sights a gun. This brings the body

(Photograph No. 3)—Correct Second Position at Table (stance)—Side View.

parallel to the cue and in natural position to line up the shot. The right arm swings freely and easily without interference with the body. The left arm is extended (and keep it straight) with the hand resting upon the table to form a bridge for the cue. (See Photograph No. 3.)

To keep your left arm out straight: This is your best guide to proper stance. You always can determine your correct position at the table by stretching your left —or "bridge hand" arm—straight out in front of you to gauge your feet position—where to stand.

To get a clearer picture of this; take a front view look at my position shown in photograph No. 4. The side-back view of correct stance is shown in photograph No. 5.

Remember that your feet should be spread slightly apart to give firmness to the stance. Your weight should be evenly divided between your feet. Be certain your body is well balanced.

Billiard players, like baseball and golf stars, have different stances. None of

7

(Photograph No. 4)—Correct Second Position at Table (stance)—Front View

the professional players have precisely the same stance, but there are certain unwritten rules which all of them observe and you will improve your game if you put the above and following rules to practice. You should use the stance in which you feel natural, but one which affords a good line of aim and places you in a position to employ the required action to best advantage. I have never found two players with identical stances.

When you have to stretch to reach a shot—stretch—but feel natural, relaxed before you deliver your stroke. Bend your body over the table to a point where you can reach the shot and feel natural about doing it. And always keep your left (bridge) arm straight in front of you.

If you are left-handed, the exact opposite in all position methods holds true, of course.

Always remember that your body should be fronting the table as much as possible for ease and position, correct aim and better delivery of stroke. Do not twist your body around in such a way that it is necessary to look over your shoul-

8

(Photograph No. 5)—Correct Position at Table (stance) for Perfect Stroke—Rear

der. Keep your head directly in line with the shot. If these preliminary directions are followed, an easy, graceful and correct position is assured. Your position at the table should be practiced until you fall into it unconsciously. You are then on your way for the second fundamental factor.

One time after I had played an exhibition in Seattle, I was instructing my opponent in correct stance. He was a very dignified and cultured gentleman, 20 years my senior, and he played quite a good game of billiards although his position at the table was bad.

A large crowd was in attendance and remained for the instructive period. One spectator, who came in late and apparently had become friends with a large bottle before appearing, insisted on climbing up a pillar, with the aid of a step-ladder, in order that he might command an unobstructed view. He made the climb in the middle of the instructions, but with considerable clatter. Once securely placed, he took a good look at what was going on and demanded quite vociferously, "Say, which one of those fellows is Hoppe?"

9

Photograph No. 6)—How to Hold Cue with Correct Grip—Side-Arm Stroke.

GRIP ON THE CUE

THE best right-hand grip on the cue to use (if you're right-handed) is illustrated in Photograph No. 6. Although you'll find an occasional exception, the best professional players employ this grip.

Only the thumb and the first finger are in actual contact with the cue—the thumb over the finger nail of the forefinger. The contact is light, but tight enough to be firm—the thumb and forefinger doing all the work to grasp the cue firmly. The middle finger sometimes barely touches the cue in the grip of the average player, but very lightly.

A good rule to follow in gripping the cue is: *Tight* —where left hand forms the bridge; *Light*—where right hand holds the cue near butt end.

The most common mistake made by both beginners and many experienced amateurs is grasping the cue in a rigid, vise-like "death" grip, which destroys gentle contact of the cue tip on the cue ball.

It also is essential that you grasp the cue as close to its "balance point" as possible, not at the extreme end. (See Diagram No. 2.) This makes a shorter bridge possible and usually results in a smooth, even stroke with the

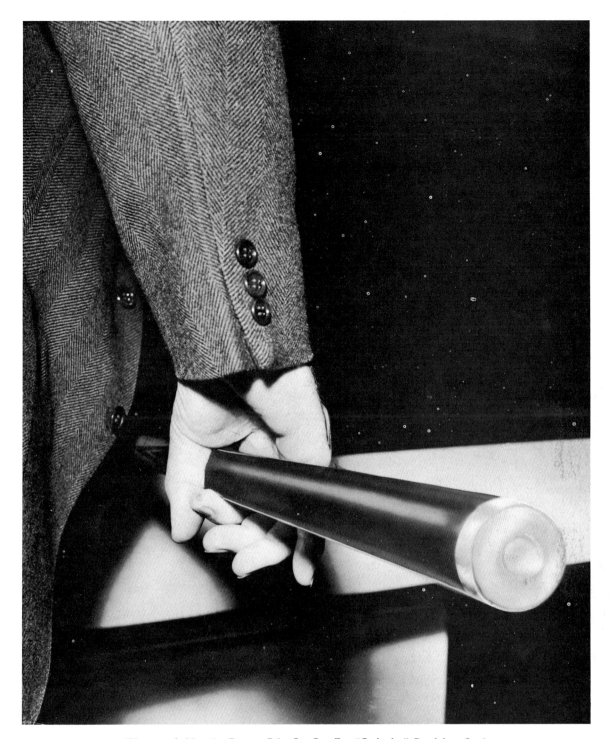

(Photograph No. 7)—Proper Grip On Cue For "Orthodox" Pendulum Stroke.

cue held level—horizontal to the table bed. (This will be fully covered in a following chapter, "Cueing the Ball.") *Remember:* Hold your cue lightly at the balance point with thumb and index finger—or both index and middle fingers—and don't try to strangle it. The cue should never be held by more than the first two fingers and the thumb. In reality, the cue simply rests on the first two fingers and is held secure by the thumb. See Photograph No. 6 (back view) again. You will notice that the upper side of the cue is not firmly against the flesh and the two small fingers are not touching the cue.

When the cue is held at its extreme end, a pump-like stroke results, in which the point of the cue dips down as it is drawn away from the ball and rises as it approaches the ball. This makes smooth execution of a shot almost impossible. Thus it becomes almost impossible to strike the cue ball accurately.

Because I started playing at such an early age that I was not tall enough to reach over the table, I learned and developed a side-arm stroke. Jake Schaefer also uses a side-arm stroke for the same reason. This motion is supposed to be one of the distinguishing marks of my play. But sometimes I doubt it.

While I was on one of my country-wide exhibition tours for the Billiard Association a few years ago, I was called to make a substitution at the last moment in a small Kansas town for Welker Cochran, then world's 3-cushion billiard champion, who had been taken ill.

I arrived just in the nick of time—a few minutes late. The proprietor of the billiard room was very excited, as a large crowd had already gathered. "My name is Willie Hoppe," I said. "I'm substituting for Welker Cochran."

The proprietor's face dropped. "Everything happens to me," he replied. "Here I have a champion booked and he can't make it. But go ahead and play—they're waiting for you—and do the best you can."

Luckily, I played well that evening. Upon conclusion of the exhibition, the still perturbed room-owner came over to me. "Thank goodness everything went all right," he sighed. "Even though you have that funny side-wheeling stroke, you play pretty good. I never heard of you," he assured me. "What did you say your name was?"

I advocate, however, the orthodox pendulum stroke. See Charlie Peterson's perfect pendulum grip as shown in Photograph No. 7. A proper follow-through can be delivered when the cue is held in this manner. This grip insures you the necessary free wrist action. It also provides action only from the elbow down when you stroke. There should be absolutely no action between your elbow and shoulder when delivering your stroke; like a clock pendulum in motion—from the elbow down—giving you free and easy wrist action.

When the pendulum stroke is used, and this is the natural one for most players, the right forearm hangs almost perpendicularly.

As greater distance is required, slip the right hand back a trifle on the butt of the cue. However, never go back to the extreme end. I play my hardest and longest shots with the cue grasped slightly back of the balance point. The weight of the cue is sufficient to secure the required driving force.

After the cue ball has been struck and your cue has followed through, you will naturally tighten your grip at the same time—and your hand will close as the stroke is completed. Your right hand, at this point, is in front of the straight down line from your elbow which will cause the cue to touch the palm of your hand and automatically tighten your grip on the butt of the cue.

This is better explained, perhaps, by reminding that when you make a stroke, the cue is brought backwards, the right hand opening slightly toward the little finger, thus keeping the cue level, and the forward stroke is completed with the hand closed around the cue.

HOLD CUE AT OR NEAR THE BALANCE.

DO NOT GRASP CUE AT BUTT END.

(Diagram No. 2)—Where, and Where Not, To Grip Cue.

Here are three Don'ts to remember regarding Gripping the Cue:

Don't hold the cue tightly in your hand.
Don't hold the cue too far forward.
Don't hold the cue too far back.

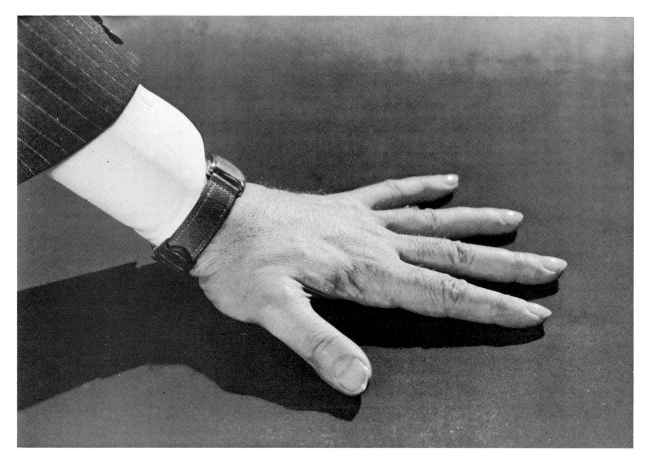

(Photograph No. 8)—Step No. 1 in Making A Bridge. Place entire hand flat on bed of table.

MAKING THE VARIOUS BRIDGES

NOTHING in fundamentals or advanced play is of greater importance than a firm bridge. The bridge forms the basis for the grip. There are variations to be found among the pros, usually due to a difference in finger lengths, but the "orthodox tripod" bridge always is the basis. The second and third fingers may be raised or lowered from this standard style of bridge to suit various shots. This will be explained later.

The execution of all shots—easy and difficult—depends on the firmness and care with which your bridge is made. It is of fundamental importance.

When you have learned to make this most common —and natural—bridge, in the right way, you are a long way along the path toward better billiards. Learn how to make a correct bridge in the very beginning and you will be doing so unconsciously after once learning how.

4-STEP METHOD

Here is the 4-step way I advise you to make your bridge: (Constantly refer to the photographs until you can make your bridge easily, quickly and comfortably.)

1. Place your entire left hand flat on the table with the heel of the hand firmly on the cloth. (See Photograph No. 8.)

2. Bend or double the forefinger until the tip rests against the thumb, forming a loop. (See Photograph No. 9.)

3. Place the cue against and in groove between thumb and forefinger as in Photograph No. 10.

4. Put the cue through the loop made by your forefinger and thumb and pull your forefinger back firmly against the cue. (See Photograph No. 11.)

You will find the second joint (doubled under) of your middle finger and the other two fingers spreading and pressing firmly against the table to form a sturdy tripod with the heel of your hand and your thumb, on the table. Don't forget to double the first joint of your middle finger back. This will give you your standard bridge as in Photograph No. 11. Incidentally, I use this type of bridge for most of my long, fast draw shots.

The cue passes through the circle of the forefinger and is guided by forefinger, thumb and middle finger. The photographs referred to above illustrate, better than words, just what I mean.

ORTHODOX TRIPOD BRIDGE

Now to form the orthodox tripod bridge, seen in Photograph No. 12, which I use and advocate for general 3-cushion play, raise the heel of the hand off the table, putting all the pressure of the hand on your thumb, curled-back middle finger and third and little finger. You can automatically sense the firmness and solidity of this bridge.

There is no firmer or better bridge possible. It really is a quadruped bridge, inasmuch as it has four base con-

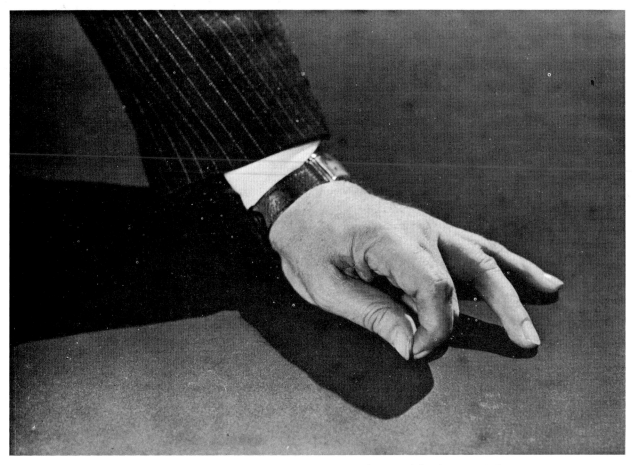

(Photograph No. 9)—Step No. 2 in Making A Bridge. Bend forefinger until the
tip rests against the thumb—forming a loop.

tact points. See two additional positions of this all-important bridge in Photographs Nos. 23 and 24 in next chapter. I suggest that you study these other hand positions as well as those you have just been over in this section. They are a little different.

BRIDGE FOR FOLLOW (ABOVE CENTER ON CUE BALL) SHOTS

The bridge for follow and above-center-on-cue-ball shots, which I often use in 3-cushion competition, is illustrated in Photograph No. 13. It gives you a side slant showing the place you want to strike the cue ball when you use this bridge.

Double the forefinger around the cue until the first joint rests against the thumb and the end of the thumb rests against the second joint of the middle finger, which provides a rest for the cue.

The points of contact with the table are the heel of the hand, the entire first joint of the little finger, the tip of the third finger, and the first joint of the middle finger.

Perhaps the best explanation of how to properly make this bridge again is told in illustrated form, so see and study the 4-step method in Photographs 8, 9, 10, and 11.

If your forefinger is not long enough to permit the first joint to be folded against the thumb, a firm bridge still may be obtained by closing the circle with the tip of the forefinger against the thumb, still holding the cue-tip firmly. Firmness and solidity is the rule in this bridge, and in all others; just as lightness is required for the cue grip with your right hand.

BRIDGE FOR DRAW SHOTS

The bridge recommended for draw shots is illustrated in Photograph No. 11 and previously explained—essentially the same in all particulars. The necessity of pulling the middle finger back under the hand is understood when you realize that the purpose is to strike the cue ball below center to make draw shots. The cue is, of course, brought lower by this method.

However, this bridge is not as low as the "fist" draw bridge, to be explained next.

To effect draw action on the cue ball and, at the same time, impart drive to the object ball—the purpose of this bridge—a longer bridge is used than in the case of a short draw and slight elevation of the butt of the cue is advisable. Length of bridges and elevations and levels of the cue will be explained in closely following paragraphs.

The same element of firmness which marks the tripod bridge is evident in this spread-draw bridge-position. When steady pressure is exerted upon the entire hand, this bridge becomes as firm as a part of the table.

The forefinger should be wrapped completely around the cue and its tip held by the thumb. Contact should be close, so that there will be no chance for the cue to "wabble" about. A common error is to permit the forefinger to go "free." The tip of the forefinger *MUST* be doubled under the thumb and firmly held.

The method of folding the forefinger and position of the other fingers as shown in Photograph No. 18—and for all other bridge styles—is easy and natural with a little practice. It can be adopted by any player, whether his fingers are long or short.

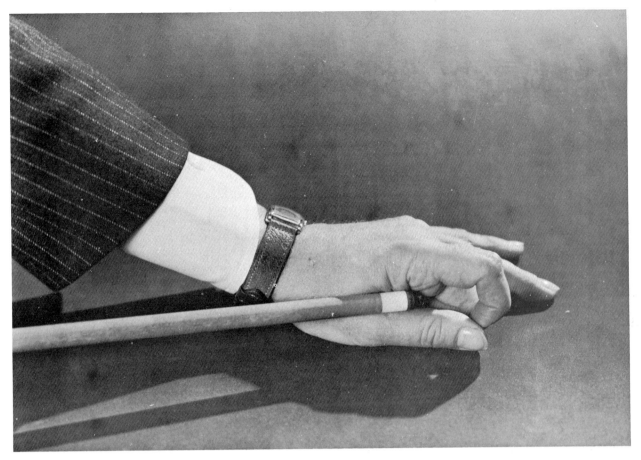

(Photograph No. 10)—Step No. 3 in Making A Bridge. Place the tip against and
in groove between thumb and forefinger.

FIST BRIDGE FOR SHORT DRAW SHOTS

Jake Schaefer, Sr., was the first of the topflight pros to use the "fist" bridge for short or "nip" draw shots. Today all the experts employ this type of bridge.

No bridge provides a firmer base than the fist bridge. The cue passes over the thumb which is resting flat on the table, and then passes between the first and second fingers, with the former (forefinger) again wrapped completely around the cue with the tip against the thumb. The other fingers are doubled up exactly as in making a fist to deliver a punch. (See Photograph No. 14.) Remember, this bridge is to be used only for draw shots and not when the object ball is to be driven around the table.

The great advantage of this simple bridge is that it affords absolute accuracy in striking the cue ball. It forces you to strike exactly where you aim. Moreover, it forces the cue down as low as is practicable. It also assures quick draw response of the cue ball.

RAIL BRIDGES

Approximately 90% of shots made with the cue ball close to, or on, the cushion should be shot with the cue almost level.

I want to emphasize this fact because I find that a constant error made by many players—beginners and experienced—is immediately elevating the butts of their cues to make shots when cue balls rest near cushions. Elevation is necessary only when a half-masse stroke is needed, or when you have to play over an object ball; neither situation being frequent. Elevation is fully ex-

plained in the following "Stroke" Chapter. The masse is discussed at close of this chapter.

Rail bridges are solid supports in which the first and second fingers, one on each side of the cue, press gently against the cue and form a slot through which the cue easily slides. When the cue ball is a short distance off the rail, use the bridge as illustrated in Photograph No. 15. When the cue ball rests against, almost against, or is frozen to the cushion, employ the bridge as shown in Photograph No. 16. Notice that the thumb is firmly braced against the outer rail to provide solidness. You will quickly see that this latter bridge brings your cue tip farther away from the cue ball, as desired. The former bridge places the cue tip closer the cue ball, as needed. The only basic difference in these bridges is, therefore, in their lengths—as required. Study them closely and you will be able to execute them easily.

The half-masse bridge—Photograph No. 17—is recommended when an object ball rests very close to the cue ball near the cushion, as shown. The fingers form the base firmness of this style of bridge with the cue resting in the outside groove formed by the thumb and forefinger. Practice this bridge until you develop solidity.

The matter of elevation is easily regulated. The top surface of the cushion and rail serves as a guide, the cue resting flat upon the rail and cushion; the cushion itself having a slightly beveled edge to perfectly direct action of the cue when it rests on it.

The rail bridges always should be used in preference to most of the insecure emergency bridges generally employed when it is necessary to distort the hand—because of the position of the cue ball—to get a bridge grip on the cue.

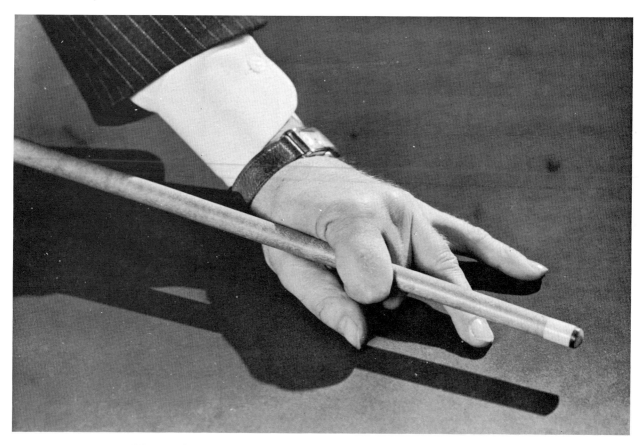

(Photograph No. 11)—Closeup of Standard Bridge. Method of folding the fore-finger and position of the other fingers.

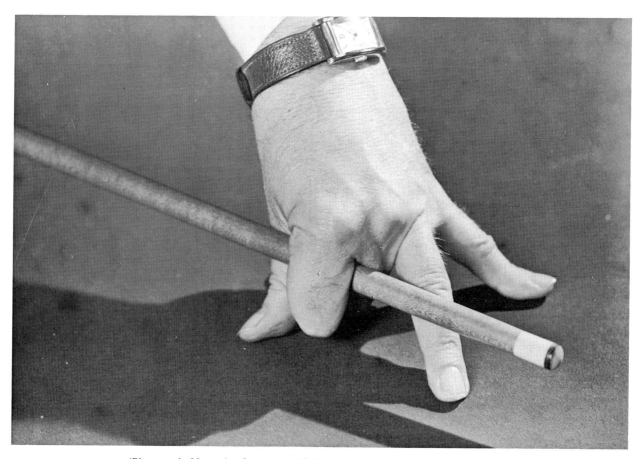

(Photograph No. 12)—Customary "Orthodox" or Common Bridge for general 3-cushion play.

(Photograph No. 13)—Bridge for Follow and Above-Center-On-Cue-Ball Shots.
Side View. Also average length of a bridge.

(Photograph No. 14)—Fist Bridge—for Short or "Nip" Draw Shots.

17

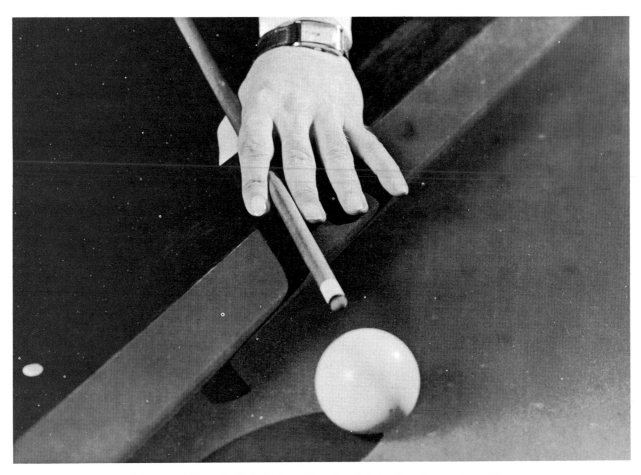

(Photograph No. 15)—Rail Bridge—When Cue Ball is off or close to the cushion.

Remember that conditions do not always make is possible to use the rail bridges illustrated, but, under most circumstances, these bridges and outlined rules of application will prove 100% efficient.

OVER-BALL BRIDGES

The bridge for shooting with the cue over another ball is formed by pressing the weight of the hand firmly on the little and middle fingers with some aid provided by the third finger against the table. This bridge (side-front view) is shown in Photograph No. 18. The cue slides in the groove provided by the curled thumb.

In another type of over-ball bridge the little and forefinger are pressed firmly against the table, with the middle and third fingers acting as secondary supports by their first joints being on the table.

The cue is placed in the groove formed by the curled up thumb and the outer part of the forefinger.

It might appear that the cue is touching the cue ball in the over-ball bridge, but if you look at the shadows on the table you will see that proper clearance is provided. Always place your bridge hand as close to the cue ball as possible in making this style of bridge, but far enough back so you won't touch or foul the cue ball, with the cue or your hand, and, of course, at a distance that your good judgment will determine to be natural and correct.

Be certain over-ball bridges are rigid and solid before delivering the stroke.

SHOOTING WITH OPPOSITE HANDS

You will often find the balls in positions difficult to reach with the customary bridges. So it is quite important for you to practice handling the cue and shooting with your left hand if you are a natural right-hander (vice-versa if you're left-handed).

You will find many shots easy to get to by using the opposite hand for bridge and grip when they are practically impossible to reach in your natural way.

My advice is to practice and learn the reverse, or unnatural, position—after you have learned the natural stance, grip and bridge fundamentals.

By being ambidextrous with the cue, you will vastly improve your game.

SUBSTITUTE BRIDGE

Very few players—novices or advanced—understand how to use the substitute bridge for their bridge hand when shots are difficult or impossible to reach naturally.

Photograph No. 19 shows you the method of handling this bridge. Carefully study its every detail as it will be of assistance to you.

The grip at the butt of the cue is almost the usual one, turned up and forward. The cue lies on the thumb with the middle and forefinger on top of it. The shaft of the substitute bridge lies flat on the table, to the left of the shot, with your left hand holding it steady. The end of the bridge is held between the middle and forefinger with the heel of the hand pressed firmly on top of it. The thumb, not shown in the photograph, also acts as a support—by being braced against the end of the wooden bridge shaft. This affords you a natural stance at the table with a well-balanced position.

18

(Photograph No. 16)—Rail Bridge—When cue ball is against, almost against, or frozen to the cushion (rail).

As a further guide, always have your line of vision directly in line with the shot—looking *straight down* the cue to the cue ball.

The head of the substitute bridge should be at a distance from cue ball to enable perfect action—the spot on cue ball you wish to strike. Any of the fine grooves in the head—or edge—of the substitute bridge can be used, depending again on where you want to strike the cue ball.

Never hold the bridge shaft off the table. This eliminates firmness, and the bridge usually moves—causing a miss. The *ONLY* time not to place the substitute bridge flat on the table is when other balls interfere and then you should shoot left-handed—or the reverse from your natural manner.

LENGTH OF BRIDGE

Possibly the greatest aid in enabling a player to strike a cue ball where he aims and to control the object balls is regulation of the length of the bridge. By this is meant the distance between the cue ball and the bridge hand.

In 3-cushions, where a great deal of length is required on many shots, the bridge should be from six to seven inches. A shot requiring unusual force sometimes demands an eight to nine inch bridge.

The average bridge length is shown in Photograph No. 13.

Long shots may require either a long or short bridge. A medium draw shot or an ordinary one-cushion shot should be played with a bridge of approximately five inches. The close nurse, or play in which the balls are moved very little, calls for a short bridge, usually from three and one-half to four inches.

The average pocket-billiards bridge is around seven inches—due to long object ball shots.

The short bridge always should be favored and used as often as possible. It enables you to strike the cue ball more accurately than if you employed a long bridge, which would allow more sway to the tip of the cue.

The longer the bridge—the greater is the danger of missing the desired point on the cue ball, and, in turn, the object ball.

Differences in style of play, stroke and bridges, etc., are very slight between the expert pros. However, I once encountered a billiard fan who could tell by sound who was playing.

I was on tour with the late George Sutton when I met this enthusiast, a World War veteran, in Omaha, Nebraska. He came with his wife to our exhibition.

He remained in his seat during the entire time we were playing our 400-point match. After the match, his wife asked me if I would come over to meet him. Naturally, I agreed and had a long chat with him. He said he thoroughly enjoyed the match.

"I love the click of the ivories," he informed me. "There is a world of difference in the sound of your play and that of Mr. Sutton's. That's the way I watch it—by sound."

The man was blind.

MASSE BRIDGES—(FOR ADVANCED PLAYERS)

Bridges for masse shots are the most difficult of all to make. The entire weight of the bridge hand and firmness of the bridge rests on the third and little fingers, with auxiliary support provided by the middle finger. Points of contact on the table are the entire tips of the third

(Photograph No. 17)—Half-Masse Bridge—When object ball is close to cue ball near a cushion.

(Photograph No. 18)—Bridge for Shooting Over a Ball. Side-Front View.

(Photograph No. 19)—Handling the Substitute Bridge—Grip and Bridge Hands.

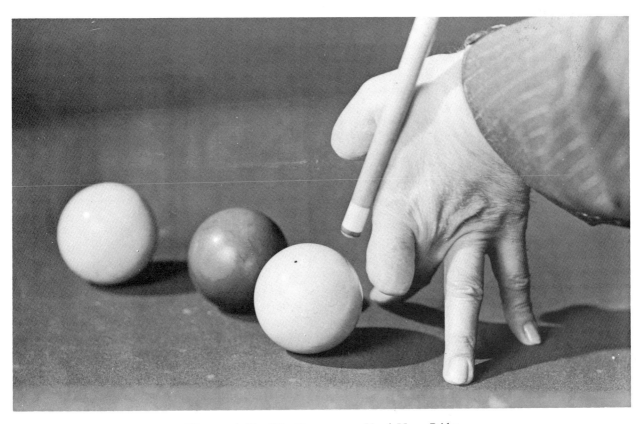

(Photograph No. 20)—Customary or Usual Masse Bridge.

(Photograph No. 21)—Grip on Cue for Masse Shots.

and little fingers and the first joint of the middle finger. See the pressure exerted on these fingers in a correct customary masse bridge position in Photograph No. 20.

Be certain to place the bridge hand fingers, as illustrated, very firmly on the table and twist the hand outward—to the left—as far as possible. This will insure a solid bridge. The forefinger and thumb are doubled under and neither should touch the table. The cue slides through in the groove formed between the curled thumb and forefinger—on the outside of the hand.

Remember: Stand facing the table as much as possible and as close to it as necessary. A good rule for position—stance—is lining up the shot in the ordinary way, determining where you'd stand and then swinging your body half-way to the right; in other words, right face; and bend body slightly forward and naturally toward the table. (See Photograph No. 22.)

Your grip on the cue for masse shots is shown in Photograph No. 21. Note that the index side of the hand is turned toward the floor and the same regular thumb-forefinger-middle finger grip contact on the cue is employed.

However, some experts use the reverse position for their cue grip on masse shots—with the little finger side of the hand facing the floor and with the cue held between the tips of the middle finger, forefinger and thumb.

The cue is held below the balance point—toward the tip end—for most masse shots. See Photograph No. 21 again for clear understanding of this point.

FREE-HAND MASSE BRIDGE (FOR ADVANCED PLAYERS)

The "free-hand" masse means a shot in which the bridge hand does not touch or rest upon the table. This is illustrated in Photograph No. 22.

(Photograph No. 22)—Entire "Free-Hand" Masse Position, Grip, Bridge and Action.

The bridge in the free-hand masse is made by forming a fist and then sliding the cue through a loop formed by the thumb and forefinger. The forefinger is completely wrapped around the cue and firmly holds the cue. (See Photograph No. 22 again.)

Inasmuch as your bridge hand doesn't touch the table, firmness is secured by keeping your arm locked against your left side with your elbow pressing tightly against the side and forearm stiff. Hold arm, wrist and hand as steady as possible.

Note shadow of cue tip on cue ball in the photograph last referred to, showing where cue tip should strike in order to make this 3-cushion free-hand masse shot.

The grip employed in free-hand masse shots is the same as in other masse grips.

The free-hand masse is used where the draw action must be extremely powerful. It requires a very steady hand because, as previously explained, neither hand touches the table for a brace.

The entire free-hand action is shown in Photograph No. 22—illustrating position at the table, grip, balance point to hold cue, bridge, slant of body and angle of cue. Correct angle of cue for these shots is discussed in a following chapter on the "Masse."

HINTS FOR BRIDGES

The main motive in making any style of bridge—holding the cue on the table—is firmness.

Avoid a long bridge.

Keep the left (or bridge) hand on the table after the cue ball is struck. In other words, the bridge hand should remain in position, without moving, a moment after the stroke has been completed to prevent what is known as body english, or twisting, which destroys accuracy.

23

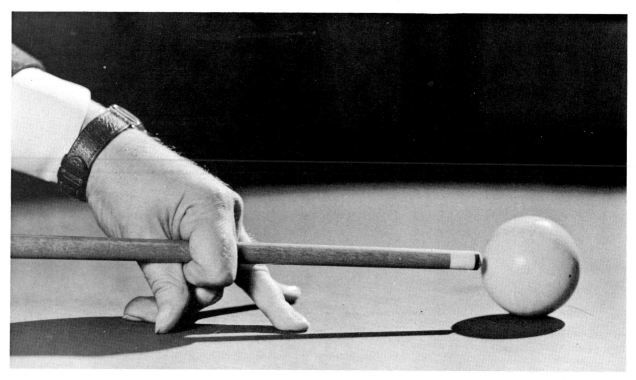

(Photograph No. 23)—Proper Place to Strike Cue Ball for Most Follow Shots.

STRIKING THE CUE BALL

KNOWN AS
CUEING (ADDRESSING) THE BALL

THE proper method of cueing the ball—striking the cue ball—is a vital fundamental next in importance to developing a good, firm bridge. You will never learn to play billiards unless you cue the ball properly.

Without a doubt the most frequent cause of poor playing and retarded improvement is incorrect cueing.

The most important point to remember in cueing or stroking the cue ball is simply: Avoid extreme english.

All professionals learned this in the beginning and when you study or watch them in action you will observe that they seldom use extreme english. English is fully explained in the following chapter.

The standard billiard ball is 2⅜ inches in diameter. If a line were drawn around the face of the ball toward the player, half way between the outer edge and the center of the ball, the circle would be approximately the size of a half dollar.

NEVER STRIKE THE CUE BALL OUTSIDE THIS IMAGINARY CIRCLE AND YOU WILL PLAY SOUND BILLIARDS. In other words, keep the entire cue tip within this circle. Since it is impossible to draw lines on the cue ball, remember this: Don't strike further out than half way between the center and the outer edge of the cue ball. Any stroke delivered outside the circle would be taking a chance—dangerous—might cause miscues and should be avoided by all means.

See Diagram No. 4 to clearly give you the picture at a glance. This diagram shows you where to strike the cue ball—the areas for the basic strokes. The drawing represents the face of the cue ball. It is not exact size, but the relative area is correctly shown.

Strokes one-half above the center of the cue ball will

produce a follow. (See Photograph No. 23. Also see Diagram No. 4, page 26.)

Strokes one-half below the center of the cue ball will produce a draw shot. (See Photograph No. 24.)

Also take careful note of the bridges in these last two photographs. They are helpful in showing you additional different views of the positions of the hand in the various bridge styles illustrated and explained in the foregoing chapter, "Making the Various Bridges."

Strokes one-half to the right of center will produce right english and strokes one-half to the left of center will produce left english. See Diagram No. 4 again for visualization of right and left english shots and where to strike the cue ball.

There are variations, of course, of side english, follow and draw shots. For instance, a stroke delivered above and to the right of center will produce both follow and right english. A stroke delivered below and to the right of center will produce both draw and right english. A stroke delivered above and to the left of center will produce both follow and left english. A stroke delivered below and to the left of center will produce both draw and left english. Again look at Diagram No. 4 for spots to strike cue ball for these four types of shots.

HITTING THE OBJECT BALL

Diagram No. 3 illustrates how the cue ball must hit the first object ball when a full ball is called for; when the shot requires a three-quarter ball contact; when it is necessary to hit the object ball one-half full, one-third full, one-quarter full; and also for four-fifths, two-thirds and very thin ball contacts.

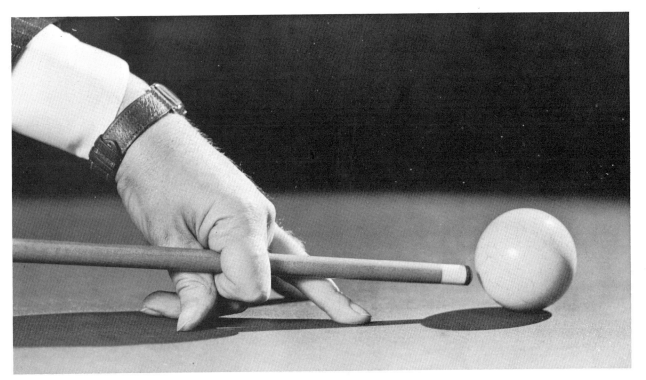

(Photograph No. 24)—Correct Place to Strike Cue Ball for Most Draw Shots.

Practice hitting the first object ball as shown in Diagram No. 3, because you later will find that your ability to do this well is a very important phase of good billiards.

The best practice you can obtain in correctly hitting the object ball is to place the cue ball close to it and then gradually increase the distance between cue ball and object balls as you become more proficient.

Remember to practice. Practice and actual experience must guide your general method of play.

ADDRESSING THE CUE BALL

I often have been asked why I dip my cue down on the cloth in front of the cue ball when addressing a shot before delivering the stroke.

The reason I do this is to afford me a clear view of the entire shot—from cue ball to object ball—where to strike cue ball, and, in turn, to hit the object ball. This is called "sighting the shot."

You can readily understand that when you drop the cue down in this manner you can see the shot before you much clearer. Of course, the cue strikes the spot on the cue ball you aim at when the stroke is delivered—with level action. This is explained in the following "Stroke" Chapter.

AIMING

Select the spots on the object and cue balls you wish to hit. Then concentrate on this line of aim—watch tip of cue in preliminary strokes to see that your tip is going to the same spot. Your eye and hand should act in strict unison.

A glance should go from the cue ball to the object ball, back to the cue ball, and rest there—so you must be looking at the cue ball, rather than the object ball before delivering your stroke.

The argument often has arisen whether or not a player's last glance before striking the cue ball is on the cue or object ball. My eyes are last on the cue ball.

However, several of my fellow pros often have wanted to bet me that I was wrong. Be that as it may, it doesn't mean a thing to better play. Both methods are satisfac-

tory. Anyway, you will do this automatically and unconsciously.

Speaking of wagering reminds me of a most humorous incident. Charlie Peterson and I were on one of our numerous tours several years ago. We landed in Spokane for an exhibition.

Before we started playing, an Indian chief, in magnificent regalia, strode up to Peterson. Evidently he thought Charlie was my manager.

"My son is a very good player," he informed Pete in excellent English. "I would like to arrange a game between Mr. Hoppe and my son at the conclusion of his

HOW TO HIT OBJECT BALL.

FULL BALL   4/5 BALL   3/4 BALL

2/3 BALL   1/2 BALL   1/3 BALL

1/4 BALL   THIN BALL.

Diagram No. 3.

match—say 250 points for a side bet of ten thousand dollars!"

Pete didn't know what to say. He knew I didn't bet on my game, neither did he. We both started to worry about how to evade the issue without appearing pikers.

We started our match without saying anything further to the chief. After the completion of the exhibition, I slyly glanced over toward where the Indians were sitting but they were gone. I happened to make a run of 246 that evening.

Which again proves—never bet a man at his own game.

APPLYING ENGLISH

ENGLISH, sometimes called twist and spin, is a term that means to strike the cue ball on one side, giving it a peculiar twisting motion that has great effect upon coming in contact with an object ball or cushion. It also affects the course of the first object ball, causing it to spin in the opposite direction from that of the cue ball that strikes it.

An object ball, in turn, imparts the reverse spin to another object ball.

Very few players—beginners and experienced—understand that excessive english is dangerous—unsound. It not only causes frequent miscues, but also influences the course of the cue ball, causing it to strike an object ball or first cushion a fraction of an inch to one side of where the player aimed. This is enough to be the difference between a point and a miss—victory and defeat.

I use as little english as possible; and only when it is absolutely necessary. Welker Cochran, Jake Schaefer, Johnny Layton and the rest of the topflight stars also use less english than the average player. And their success speaks for itself. They know the value of "center ball" for accuracy and have learned the lesson by constant practice.

All players should profit by their and my experience, gained through more than two score years. The greatest exponent of center ball 3-cushion play was the late Augie Kieckhefer, many times world's champion at the angle style game.

Approximately 80% of shots can be made by cueing the ball in the center. However, since it is almost impossible for any player to strike the cue ball in the exact center every time he strokes, it is advisable to use a very slight favoring english, follow and draw as explained in last chapter, "Cueing the Ball."

In applying english, I repeat—never cue the ball at a spot more than one-half of the radius of the ball from the center.

See Diagram No. 4 for basic stroking area. Follow is accomplished by striking the ball at point "A," and all strokes above the line E-D will produce a follow shot. Draw is obtained by striking the ball at point "B," and all strokes below the line E-D will effect a draw shot. Right or left english is acquired by striking the cue ball at points "D" or "E," respectively; therefore, all strokes to the right of line A-B will produce english for the right side and

strokes to the left of the A-B line will result in english to the left side.

Strict adherence to this practice will eliminate 75% of miscues and enable you to hit the object ball at least 50% more effectively.

A valuable point to remember, which will be an aid in 3-cushion play and will be fully explained in following "Science" Chapter, is that putting extreme english on the cue ball from the center of the table and hitting the center

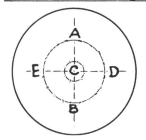

HOW TO STRIKE CUE BALL.

STROKES ABOVE LINE E-D PRODUCE A FOLLOW SHOT.

STROKES BELOW LINE E-D PRODUCE A DRAW SHOT.

STROKES RIGHT AND LEFT OF LINE A-B PRODUCE ENGLISH.

FAVORING- TOP, BELOW, RIGHT AND LEFT WITHIN INNER CIRCLE C.

Diagram No. 4.

diamond on a short rail will bring your cue ball to the center diamond on a long rail. This is the very *EXTREME* of english.

I haven't an exact rule for the use of english. Practice will soon teach you the approximate amount of english necessary. It may be needless to advise that if the cue ball is to spin to the right, right english is used, and vice versa.

ALWAYS REMEMBER: USE AS LITTLE ENGLISH AS POSSIBLE.

STROKE AND FOLLOW-THROUGH

IN WATCHING young players to discover some who may be worthy of special attention, I am immediately attracted to those who have an even, rhythmic stroke, with a clean follow-through. All experts are likewise attracted. Show me a player with a good stroke and I'll show you a good billiard player; if not at the moment, then in the very near future.

To acquire a good, even stroke, you *must,* above all things, control your cue after coming in contact with the cue ball. Here are a few *axioms* on stroke which will prove helpful.

1. Hold your cue level—as nearly parallel to the table bed as possible. The few times that elevation is necessary (slightly raising your grip-hand) are explained a few paragraphs later. Avoid, whenever possible, shooting down at the cue ball, as in a good natural stroke the cue has a tendency to dip anyway. Keep a level cue—as nearly parallel with the table as possible.

2. Follow-through the cue ball, regardless of whether the stroke is center ball, or is to impart follow, draw, or english.

3. Finish your stroke with the cue point two, three, four or more inches beyond the place where the cue ball rested, depending on the force (speed) of the required stroke—the necessary distance to drive the cue ball or first object ball. *Follow-through!* Speed and force are explained in the following chapter.

4. *Leave your cue on the line of aim and leave your bridge-hand on the table until after the stroke is fully completed!* See Photographs Nos. 25 and 26 and also 27, 28, and 29, showing my complete stroke—from start to finish.

The finish of your stroke and follow-through is vividly illustrated in Photographs Nos. 27, 28 and 29. The two object balls in these three photos are placed there for the express purpose of showing you just how far the cue should follow-through on the majority of shots. Also notice the tendency of the cue to dip down toward the table. This proves how the cue tip cuts into the cue ball and why you should hold your cue as level as possible to avoid jump.

5. *Never* permit the cue tip to waver about in the air after delivering your stroke. Always follow-through on

(Photograph No. 25)—Correct Stroke in Second Motion—at back-swing extreme.

(Photograph No. 26)—Correct Stroke in Third and Final Movement.—Finish of
follow-through; leaving cue on line of aim and bridge-hand on table after contact
with cue ball.

each stroke! This is as important in billiards as in any other sport.

6. *Never* permit the cue tip to slide off to the right or left when putting english on the cue ball. Follow straight through.

While it is true that the cue tip is in contact with the ball only for a tiny fraction of a second, the straight, clean follow-through will influence the course of the cue ball to an infinite extent, as it prolongs the contact that can't be seen with the naked eye.

7. I have seen many players display the fault of pulling or swinging their cues in the direction in which they wish to impart english. It's a dangerous fault and should never be started. I have seen this mistake made by several experts from time to time in world championship competition. I hope by this time that they have corrected their mistake.

There's no need ever to start this practice; no need ever to make a miscue by doing it and then, for lack of a better excuse, to take a look at the cue tip and say, "Give me a file."

As Jake Schaefer, Sr., once told me, "Son, it's not those balls, table, and your cue that are supposed to be smart,—it's you."

PRACTICE STROKE

You should take at least two or three practice or preliminary strokes to the cue ball before striking it. In other words, you should "fiddle" a couple of strokes to obtain proper force and precision before striking the cue ball. This develops a better stroke, as well as better assuring you of striking where you aim. The final stroke is faster, the added speed being the result, more than any other one thing, of the quick snappy action of the wrist.

Practice your stroke with only the cue ball, striking it squarely in the center and delivering a quick, but not too hard, impact and straight follow-through, with your cue left on the line of aim.

Naturally, the length of your stroke on the backswing is the length of your bridge; and on the forward swing it is the combined distance of the length of your bridge and your follow-through.

There are three movements in the stroke—addressing the cue ball; backswing; and follow-through. (See Photographs Nos. 25 and 26 again.)

The stroke of the cue should resemble the action of a pendulum—perfectly even—with the last stroke made like the preliminary strokes, except that you go into the cue ball slightly quicker than in just addressing it with practice motions.

To acquire command of the cue, and to learn to strike the cue ball accurately, the following practice is advised. Place the cue ball about 18 inches from the head of the table and in a direct line with the middle diamonds at the foot and head of the table. Aim at the middle diamond at the foot of the table and try to make the ball return in the same line and hit the end of the cue, which

(Photograph No. 27)—Start of Correct Follow-through Stroke.

(Photograph No. 28)—Mid-way in Proper Follow-through Stroke; after cue has struck cue ball.

(Photograph No. 29)—Finish of Correct Follow-through Stroke. This shows the extreme, with cue following through approximately eight inches after striking cue ball.

(Photograph No. 30)—Correct Position for Elevation of the Cue Stroke.

is left in follow-through position after the stroke. The accurate return of the cue ball can be accomplished only by striking the ball exactly in the vertical line through its center, and you quickly learn how accurate your stroke must be.

Notice that the direction of the ball on rebounding is unchanged whether it is struck at dead center or a cue tip above or below this point, so long as it is struck vertically in the middle. But, with the least variation from this middle line, it comes back to the right or left of its original path.

Also, when struck below the center, it slows up somewhat as it goes down the table. A cue ball struck at dead center, or a little below, runs more truly than when struck above this point; and, consequently, the center stroke should be used in the majority of ordinary or usual shots.

This practice stroke should be repeated with various speeds until it can be executed with uniform success. Speed of stroke is fully covered in the following chapter.

ALWAYS REMEMBER: Hold the cue as nearly parallel to the table as possible, for all shots except those explained in following "Elevation of the Cue" paragraphs.

Take another look at Stance Photographs Nos. 1, 2, 4 and 5, especially No. 5 for rear-side view, showing perfect stroke action in your position at the table.

ELEVATION OF THE CUE

The only times you should elevate the butt of your cue from the usual level position, (See Photograph No. 30 for a vivid description of what is meant by cue elevation) is when playing one of the following shots:

1. Driving an object ball around the table for distance or position.

2. Dead-ball draw or follow, when the first object ball is driven to a cushion, or for putting speed on an object ball and killing the speed of the cue ball.

3. Cross-table, when no english is used. Elevation results in a wider (greater) angle from the first cushion. Provides a straighter angle with no swing, and you go through the cue ball better.

4. When curve is desired on around-the-table shots. That is, when a swing in the angle (not a stationary straight line) to object ball or cushion is needed in going around the table.

5. When an object ball is on the cushion. Elevation enables you to go through the ball better in this type of shot and provides the necessary curve from the ball and rail to correctly go around the table. Eliminates the possibility of coming out straight from a ball on the cushion.

6. And, of course, in the use of the masse or half-masse.

Elevation of the butt of your cue in these cases enables you to go through the cue ball better and, in turn, to go through an object ball or cushion sharper—better.

My parting advice on stroke is to take close study of my elevation stroke in Photograph No. 30, and then compare it with photos showing my natural, regular stroke.

SPEED AND FORCE

SPEED of your stroke and, in turn, of the cue ball is paramount. It is very important for you to remember that the speed with which you shoot has much to do with the action of your cue ball after contact with an object ball or cushion.

For instance, if you use extra speed, your cue ball will leave the object ball at a shorter angle than if you were to shoot easy. Many shots are missed because they are played too hard or easy. Knowing the action of the balls at various speeds, both with and without coming in contact with the cushions, is an essential part of good billiard play.

I group speeds into three classes: easy, moderate, and hard. Practice striking the cue ball and classify this trio of speeds according to your especial stroke.

The effect of english, as of all rotations,—follow and draw—is modified by the speed of the ball; for the natural progressive motion of the cue ball is always one component in the final result. The greater the speed in this direction, the less will be the deflection from rotational forces.

The main thing to remember in speed simply is: Slow speed widens the angle; fast speed narrows the angle. Therefore, in the majority of shots, if a short angle is desired, shoot with a moderate or hard stroke; if a long angle is required, strike the cue ball with an easy or easy-moderate stroke.

The best way I have found out how to determine speed is the distance you follow-through the cue ball. Therefore, I advise you to practice to determine how far *YOU* must follow-through to obtain easy, moderate or hard speeds. The evenness of your stroke also is important. (See Diagram No. 5:—"C" denotes a hard stroke for fast speed; "B" signifies a moderate stroke for average speed; and "A" shows an easy stroke for slow speed—with long, medium and short follow-through, respectively, denoted by arrows on far side of the cue balls. These follow-throughs are approximately eight, five and three inches.)

In playing for position, the strength of the stroke is important, since the final positions of all three balls are largely influenced by it. The places where the balls come to rest depend upon their speed quite as much as on their direction.

The force which an object ball receives is the result of two factors: (1) The point of impact with the cue ball; (2) The speed.

The speed of the cue ball is modified by the place it hits the object ball. Striking an object ball full naturally will slow it up more than striking one thin. In the same manner, english affects the speed of the cue ball after striking a cushion.

A ball with english or follow will go further than a ball without english after it hits an object ball or cushion because the spin carries it forward in its path. Similarly, a ball with reverse english or draw action slows up after impact. These effects are readily understood by playing at a moderate pace, nearly full on an object ball, with follow and natural english, and then repeating the shot with draw and reverse english.

Two factors should be deliberately considered in planning position shots; at what point and with what force the object ball should be hit to bring it to the desired position, and what effect and speed must be given the cue ball in order to make the shot when the object ball is struck in this manner.

Incidentally, it is of interest to you to observe the distance which a ball travels with strokes of different lengths, as a gauge of the force to be employed in various shots. The maximum distance, of course, varies on different tables, but it will be found that on ordinary tables the cue ball can be made to traverse the table length about four times on hard strokes.

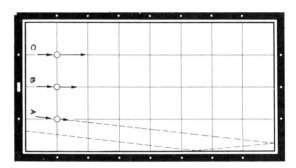

Diagram No. 5.

The "lag" or "bank" shot (to determine who shoots first) naturally depends on follow-through. There is no better place to explain the lag than here.

"A" in Diagram No. 5 shows the shot known as lagging or banking for the break. I strike the cue ball one-half cue tip above direct center with about a five inch even follow-through stroke. (This shot is not drawn to proportion on the diagram, so disregard the length of this lag follow-through as shown in comparison to Shots "B" and "C." The length of the lag follow-through would more resemble Shot "B.") I aim to hit the far rail with the cue ball about one-quarter of a diamond from the corner, which brings it down the table just below the second diamond on the long rail and—if played perfectly—will bring the cue ball against the cushion at the head of the table. If this is accomplished—the worst you could get out of a lag like this would be a tie.

Which reminds me of an often-discussed and noteworthy incident, inasmuch as a lag was instrumental in the present world's 18.2 balkline high run record.

Back in 1926 at Chicago, Jake Schaefer, Jr., and Erich Hagenlacher met for the championship. They were both nervous and wanted the other to shoot first. So they lagged and both banks were terrible—landing in the middle of the table. Charlie Peterson, the referee, squinted, measured and finally awarded the bank to Schaefer.

Jake, thinking he was unlucky, broke and ran out the widely known 400 record run without missing, for the game and title. Hagenlacher never got to shoot.

The real story behind this record performance never before has been told. After the game, Peterson asked Jake why he banked so poorly. "I did so on purpose," replied Jake, "I was a little nervous and wanted Erich to start the game." Hagenlacher, overhearing the discussion, said, "Ach, I did the same thing. I vanted to lose the bank so Shake vould shoot first. I, too, was nervous."

What do you think of that? A world title at stake and neither one of these great players knew, or else both entirely overlooked, the fact that the winner of the lag has the option of shooting first or requesting his opponent to take the opening shot. And a remarkable world record resulted!

CAROMS

KNOWING how to make caroms is the most important phase of billiards. In fact, it is billiards. Whether it's straight-rail, balk-line, 3-cushions, or pocket billiards, unless you can make caroms you'll never become a good billiard player.

In 3-cushions, a carom may mean driving the cue ball from the first object ball to a cushion, or it may mean driving the cue ball from the cushions to the first object ball. The all-important thing, regardless of the carom position, is to stroke the cue ball properly and make certain it strikes the object cushion or ball—the way you planned it. Practice light, moderate, and hard strokes, because speed is paramount.

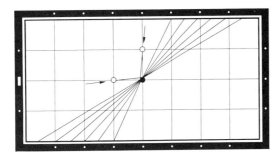

Diagram No. 6.

For example, in 3-cushions, if the cue ball is driven to the first object ball, it must carom off that ball to the exact spot on the cushion which will send it against the second and third cushions to complete the point.

If you cannot make the correct carom from an object ball to the first cushion, you have no scientific assurance that your cue ball will hit the other two cushions and the second object ball. To perfect this technique, place an object ball on the table and try to carom the cue ball from it to different points on the cushions and at different angles. By doing this, you will find your mastery of half-ball, quarter-ball, three-quarter-ball shots etc. effective. Practice them constantly and be guided by the diamonds on the rails. (See Diagram No. 6.)

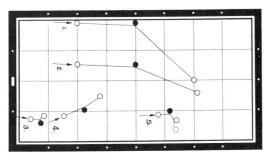

Diagram No. 7.

When a shot calls for hitting a cushion before the first object ball, it is actually easier to make the shot, but you must know where to hit the cushion. Always aim to go "through" a cushion diagonally to the point you want to hit. (See "Through" and "At" Diamond Diagram in later "Diamond System" section.)

Understand the english you put on the cue ball, and, above all, drive the ball into the cushion with true aim. Follow through!

Don't underestimate the value of caroms in 3-cushions or any other style of billiards. Caroms are the difference between making and missing shots—between victory and defeat—all other phases having been executed correctly.

CAROM SHOTS IN STRAIGHT-RAIL, ETC.

To make a "plain carom," when the balls are at an obtuse angle, as in Shot No. 1 in Diagram No. 7, hit the first object ball one-half full. To determine a half-ball, the cue ball is aimed through the edge of the first object ball, one-half of the cue tip pointing outside of the edge of the first object ball and one-half inside the edge of the first object ball.

To make a carom at a more obtuse or wider angle, as in Shot No. 2 in the same diagram, the first object ball naturally must be hit "thinner." An easy way to determine this is to point one-half full and then switch the cue so it points just outside the edge of the first object ball.

For all long caroms, like Shot No. 1, the cue ball

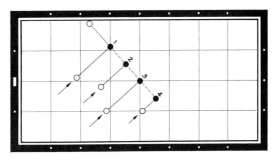

Diagram No. 8.

should be struck above the center to avoid any draw effect, holding the right hand as low as possible. Strike the cue ball at moderate speed. If it is struck hard, it will "spring" out of its natural course.

To make a carom as in Shot No. 3, and "nurse" or hold the ball, strike the cue ball very light and very low, as hitting low kills the speed. For all nursing, such as in this shot, use a very short (4 inch) bridge, and hold your cue grip hand slightly higher for these particular shots, to allow your cue to strike low with the short bridge. Never hit a slow ball in these instances, but use a quick stroke, because in close play, the balls might "freeze" or "roll off" with a slow ball. Don't use english, as english gives extra motion to the balls and makes nursing more difficult.

When the object balls are at an angle of about 45 degrees (Shot No. 1), always hit the first object ball one-half full. If the angle is sharper than 45 degrees, it is no longer a carom and the "draw shot" must be used. (See following "Draw Shot" Chapter.)

Shot No. 4 in this same diagram is a very thin shot, and is made by striking your cue ball below center with no english; just hitting the extreme edge of the first object ball. The stroke is not hard, but quick. This shot is used in preference to the "Follow shot," (See following chapter, "Follow Shot") when the object balls are not farther away than 15 inches from the cue ball. The follow shot would necessitate a long "drive" and drives are used only as a last resort.

Use absolutely no english for above Shots No. 1 and No. 2. English is unnecessary for a plain carom and is very seldom necessary for the other "ball-to-ball" shots, which are draws and follows. English is used for caroms only when it is necessary to pass the second object ball, as per dotted line in Shot No. 5. English, however, is applied in one, two, and three-cushion caroms, as explained in following chapters.

The best example of using no english, or very, very little, is shown in Diagram No. 8. These four illustrated shots, all identical in principle—the only difference being the first object ball's distance from the cue ball—are known as "right-angle" shots.

These shots, Nos. 1, 2, 3 and 4, are perfect examples of ball-to-ball caroms. They are made by hitting the object ball three-fourths or four-fifths full, towards the left, of course. Strike the cue ball in direct center, and it will carom evenly and easily to the second object ball.

It is advisable to slightly favor left-hand english on this shot, if you do not regularly count by striking your cue ball in the direct center. When the shot is missed by striking your cue ball direct center, you are not striking where you aim. Therefore, favoring to the left is recommended.

It is correct to play the shot either way and both ways should be mastered. However, play this type of shot the way you make it the greatest number of times. Employ a moderate, follow-through stroke with cue held level.

Practice this type of shot, as it represents the ideal method to learn ball-to-ball caroms and comes up in play most frequently. When you have become proficient at caroms, you then are ready for the following advanced instructions.

FOLLOW SHOTS

THE follow is one of the game's fundamental shots, coming up in all styles of play—3-cushions, straight-rail, balkline, pocket-billiards, etc. The majority of shots are in some form of follow action, so you must realize its importance and have a thorough knowledge of this type of shot. Follow, as already explained, is produced by stroking the cue ball above the center line, with a level cue, and following through. Striking the cue ball at this correct spot and in this proper manner insures you good, solid and effective contact. By cueing too high, you do not get the necessary accuracy and action that you should secure even if you are lucky enough to first escape a miscue.

Keep in mind that you do not have to strike the cue ball as near the top as possible to make a follow shot. See Photograph No. 23 again. It shows where you should strike the cue ball to effect a follow. Again, never cue more than the width of your cue tip above center and have your bridge at a proper height so that you deliver your stroke with the cue as near level as possible. Use the follow bridges illustrated in Photographs Nos. 12 and 13 at all times.

There never should be any doubt in your mind regarding the precise spot on the first object ball which you must hit in order to make a shot.

Here is my system of determining that point:

As shown in Diagram No. 9, I draw a line from the center of the second object ball through the center of the first object ball. My point of aim ALWAYS is the place on the side of the first object ball where this imaginary line A-B cuts the surface.

In this diagram, the point of aim is the spot "A" for all three variations of the follow shot represented by cue ball numbers one, two and three.

Whenever a follow shot is required, this method can be employed. The angle may be narrow or broad, but the result will be the same.

As in the draw shot, I want to impress upon you that I determine the point of aim, not the point of contact. This is fully explained in the following chapter, "Draw Shots" graphically in Diagrams Nos. 12, 13 and 14. Study this important point carefully because it will be of much value.

Always hold the cue level and at the balance point in delivering your stroke—with a firm bridge. The cue ball should be struck one-half above direct center, without english, with a full follow-through moderate stroke.

SPEED TO EMPLOY

The course your cue ball takes after contact with the first object ball in follow shots depends a great deal on the amount of speed with which you shoot.

Play ordinary follow shots with a moderate stroke—medium follow-through—for average speed. This will insure an accurate follow. It is not necessary to shoot hard to obtain follow action on the usual follow shot.

If you use too much speed, the angle your cue ball takes from the first object ball will be lengthened outward from the second object ball and, of course, you will miss the shot. *AND AVOID ENGLISH AS MUCH AS POSSIBLE.*

Try the same follow shot at various speeds and note the difference in direction of the cue ball after contact with the first object ball.

Other follow methods, shown in Diagram No. 10, are:

To make the follow as in Shot One, use center ball, no english and aim the cue ball at the center of the first object ball, then switch towards the second object ball as little as possible. Be certain the switch is done on the first object ball and not on the cue ball, thus avoiding all english. It cannot be impressed too strongly that ball-

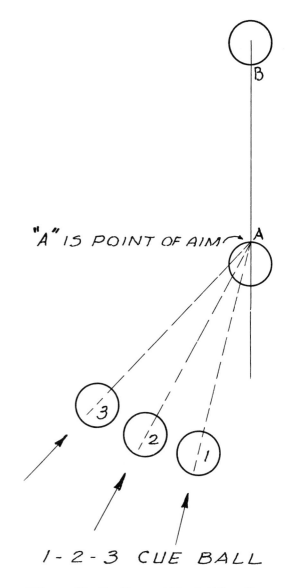

(Diagram No. 9)—How to Make A Follow Shot.

Draw a line from the center of the second object ball to the center of the first object ball—A-B. The point of aim is a spot on the far side of the first object ball where the imaginary line cuts the surface, represented by "A". Whenever a follow is indicated, this system can be employed if—you hold cue at balance; make firm bridge; use no english; strike cue ball ½ above center; and follow through with a moderate stroke.

to-ball shots (meaning where no cushion is used) need no english. The right hand (grip on cue) also must be held as low as possible.

All follow shots should be played with an easy stroke, so the object balls will be left in front of the cue ball. If the balls are struck hard, the result generally is unsatisfactory, with the cue ball in the undesirable middle position. Line-follows, when the cue ball is far from the first object ball, like long-draws, are not considered "good billiards," it being much better to use one or more cushions, as the occasion demands. This will be fully explained later, in One, Two, and Three-Cushion Carom Chapters.

To make the cushion-follow, as in Shot Two, drive the first object ball between cushion and second object ball, as per dotted line, and send cue ball to cushion and then to second object ball. Use center ball with plenty of right english. All this type of shots should be made with only moderate speed, to give the cue ball a chance to take all the necessary english. Try to drop the first object ball near the side rail, thus keeping the object balls in front of the cue ball. These shots should be practiced at the opposite end of the table, too.

Shot No. 3 is termed a dead-draw, as all the speed is given to the first object ball; the cue ball just counting on the second object ball. If played correctly, the balls should be left together. The first object ball is driven as the dotted line indicates, which brings it back to the second object ball. The cue ball is aimed full at the center of the first object ball, then switched very little from the center to the right. Strike the cue ball absolutely in the center to prevent it from following forward or drawing back. This is a good shot for practicing your stroke and position at the table, as it is easy to learn, and the mind then can concentrate on these two requisites for good billiards.

To make the follow as in Shot Four, aim at the point on the first object ball which is nearest the second object ball, as shown by dotted line; use no english, and strike cue ball one-half cue tip above direct center.

Pay no attention to point of contact in diagram — as it is drawn for clarity's sake. The best way to play the shot with the balls in this exact position would be a plain carom, although "position" might be sacrificed. The follow, in this case, is not practical billiards, any more than draw shots are, because the cue ball is too far from the first object ball.

The dead-ball follow, as shown in Shot Five of the same No. 10 Diagram, is made by striking the cue ball as close to the center as possible and still make the cue ball go forward, as explained in Diagram No. 9. This shot is mostly used for drive-shots, when the masse or cushion-carom is not practical.

FORCE-FOLLOWS

The ability to use the follow when the cue ball is close to the first object ball is difficult — accomplished by few players — mainly because they don't know how to execute this shot. But you can become proficient at making this shot, known as a force-follow, if you follow instructions and overcome the fear of miscueing.

Force-follows are used when the first object ball and cue ball are only three inches or less apart, measuring from the inside of the balls, and follow action is necessary to reach the second object ball.

One of the few times you do not use the usual follow-through stroke is in shooting force-follows. You must deliver a short, snappy, clean stroke to travel any distance at all to the second object ball — in order not to make the illegal and often debated push shot.

The way you can distinguish a push shot from a legitimate force-follow is simple: If the shot is correctly executed, the cue ball will momentarily stop, after impact

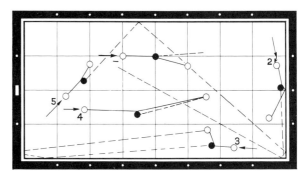

Diagram No. 10.

with the first object ball, before picking up its follow action and gaining rapid speed after its slight halt.

Be certain your cue is as near level as possible and strike the cue ball one-half cue tip above center with a short, sharp stroke. Your cue must not go through very far beyond the location of the cue ball in delivering the stroke.

Take a few preliminary strokes and then go into the cue ball according to the above directions. You soon will learn how to deliver this kind of forceful stroke when very little distance is available.

The secret in force-follows is learning where and when to quickly stop your cue after it strikes the cue ball. The best way to do this is to tighten your grip on the butt of the cue just as it strikes the cue ball, instead of the usual gradual method in the regular follow-through.

Go into this follow shot like any other. Don't check your stroke too soon and don't have fear of making a push shot — you can't, if you follow these instructions. Also don't expect to become proficient at force-follow in two or three attempts. Practice it a great deal with the balls at different distances. You soon will get results.

If you thoroughly learn the fundamentals as you come to them, practice and apply them, success will come much faster. Practicing follow shots is a step in the right direction.

DRAW SHOTS

YOU'LL never become very proficient without knowing how to make draw shots. It is part of your game's backbone. While you are called upon to execute various draw shots more in straight-rail, balkline and pocket play, don't overlook their value in 3-cushions. You will realize this more and more as you practice and progress.

As previously explained, draw action on the cue ball is produced by striking it below center. The cue should follow through on a level line, at least two or three inches past the point where the cue ball rested at the beginning of your stroke.

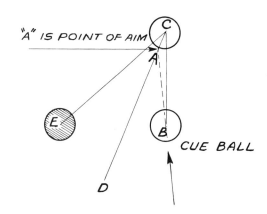

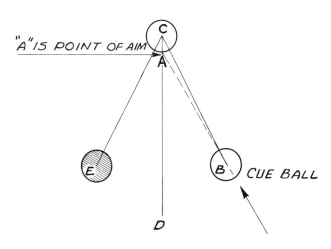

(Diagram No. 11)—How to Make A Draw Shot.

Both variations identical except in position of the balls. The lines E-C and B-C connect the centers of balls. The line C-D divides the angle between the balls. This line meets the surface of the first object ball at point A, the bisecting spot between the cue ball and the second object ball. This is the point of aim. The line of aim is represented by the line B-A. Hold cue at the balance. Make a firm bridge. Strike cue ball one-half below center. Use no english. Follow through with moderate stroke.

Determining the exact spot on the first object ball that must be hit to score the point is sometimes a confusing problem — if never explained.

The easiest system, and one I heartily recommend, is *bisecting the angle formed by the three balls.* I fully explain this in the two variations of draw shots detailed in Diagram No. 11.

Visualize an angle between the CENTERS of the three balls in each shot, the cue ball B, the first object ball C, and the second object ball E. In other words, draw an imaginary triangle from the center of the cue ball to the center of the first object ball, and from there to the center of the second object ball.

BISECT the angle BCE with the line C-D. Then aim through the CENTER of the cue ball to the point A on the first object ball. Point A is, of course, equally distant from the two sides of the triangle — the exact spot where the angle-dividing line crosses the surface of the first object ball.

Close study of the two shots (the same in principle) in Diagram No. 7 makes this clear. Let's go over it again — because you must learn to make the draw shots, and by practicing these two shots you'll learn easily and quickly:

The lines E-C and B-C connect the centers of the balls. The line C-D divides the angle between the balls. This line meets the surface of the first object ball at Point A — the bisecting point between the cue ball and first object ball. So Point A is the point of aim. The line of aim is represented by the line B-A. Hold your cue at the balance. Make a firm bridge. Strike cue ball one-half below center. Use no english. Follow-through with a moderate stroke.

By point of aim, I do not mean point of contact. As a matter of fact, point of contact is not the same, but the point of aim just described, properly used, will mean the shot will be executed.

POINTS OF AIM AND CONTACT

Study Diagrams Nos. 12, 13 and 14 and their accompanying explanations for full description of point of aim and point of contact. It is invaluable information. No matter from what part of the table the cue ball comes,

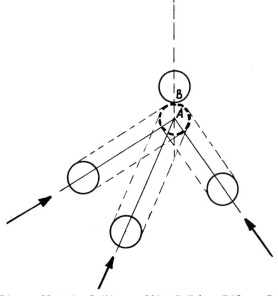

(Diagram No. 12)—Striking an Object Ball from Different Positions. In every case, the cue ball must go over the point "A" to drive the object ball in the straight upward path, represented by the vertical dotted line.

the center of the cue ball always must go over the point "A" in Diagram No. 12.

To cause the center of the cue ball to travel over the point "A" in Diagram No. 14 is the entire secret of point of aim. You can readily see that this point of aim — straight alignment of the cue in the right direction — differs from the point of contact as vividly illustrated by point "A" in Diagram No. 13.

The point "A" in Diagram No. 14 is, of course, half a ball's diameter from the object ball.

Inasmuch as Point "A" always is imaginary, there is nothing but knowledge and a keen eye to locate it.

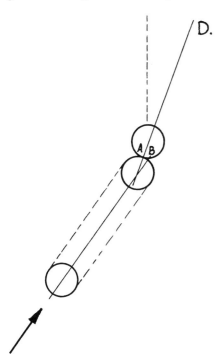

(Diagram No. 13)—The object ball can only travel in the upward dotted line path when hit at "B". If aim is taken at "B", the contact will be at "A", and the object ball will travel in the direction of "D". The parallel intersected lines denote the path of the cue ball when aim is taken at "B", and the cue ball also is shown in contact with the object ball.

By all means, understand this point of aim and contact and use it. Very few players do, and their failure to is the main reason for "over" or "under-cutting" object balls in making caroms of any kind.

The process of dividing the angle with the eye may prove difficult at first, but if you give it real attention, you soon will get the idea. After a little practice, you will see the point of aim and visualize the point of contact instinctively.

KEEP YOUR EYE LEVEL

In attempting draws, don't be afraid you'll miscue. Lower your bridge hand so when you strike the cue ball your cue is on a level. (See Photograph No. 24.) Photograph No. 24 shows where you should strike the cue ball to effect a draw.

Do not raise your bridge in making draw shots, as this causes incorrect backward action — push instead of draw — by the cue going down through the cue ball. If you employ a high bridge and downward stroke in trying to draw a ball, the cue ball will actually be driven into the table bed, causing it to jump—rebound from the cloth. Result—lost accuracy, incorrect action, and, maybe a miscue. Moreover, this practice prevents follow-through by the cue's touching the cloth. The de-

sired backspin is obtained by level cue and low bridge. The cue has a natural tendency to shoot down through the cue ball in the first place. (See Photographs Nos. 25, 26, 27, 28, and 29.) AND DON'T CUE MORE THAN THE WIDTH OF YOUR CUE TIP BELOW CENTER.

Use the draw bridges, illustrated in Photographs Nos. 11, 12 and 14, at all times.

Therefore: (1) With your bridge lower, you can strike the cue ball lower without fear of miscue. (2) By shooting with a level cue, more of the ball's weight (resistance) is in contact with the cue tip. (3) You create more backspin by shooting into a cue ball with a level cue than by shooting downward from an elevated cue angle caused by a high bridge.

Also of vast importance is the length of your bridge. Use the shortest bridge possible — determined by constant practice—in all draw shots. By doing this, you can readily understand that you'll obtain the proper follow-through. If your bridge hand is too far away from the cue ball, the cue tip will hit the cloth too soon for a clean follow-through stroke.

So move your hand closer to the cue ball when making a low bridge for draw shots. This is important for you to remember.

SPEED

Knowledge of the value of different speeds to impart to the cue ball in draw shots must be learned. It is as important for accuracy as in follow shots.

So remember the advice given as to speed in the foregoing "Follow Shots" chapter. It applies in entirety to draw shots. Then practice different speeds with the same draw shot setup. Don't employ too much force — it's unnecessary.

Two other variations of draw shots are shown in Diagram No. 15. Shot No. 1 in this diagram is known as a right-angle or "dead-ball" draw. (See Glossary of Terms at end of book.) It is made by striking the first object ball three-fourths or four-fifths full toward the left

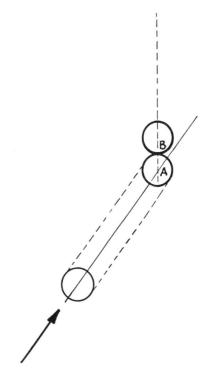

(Diagram No. 14)—The object ball can only travel in the straight upward direction when hit at "B" (contact). In order that contact may be made at "B", the alignment of the cue (aim) must be in the direction of the point "A", which point is half the diameter of a ball from "B".

37

and striking the cue ball one cue tip below center without english.

Shot No. 2 in Diagram No. 15 is known as a spread-draw. Divide the angle as for the two shots in Diagram No. 11. Again strike cue ball one-half below center — no english. The cue ball will follow the dotted line.

In both of the above shots, hold your cue level and follow-through with a moderate stroke. Use a short bridge in order to strike the cue ball exactly where you must — one-half below center.

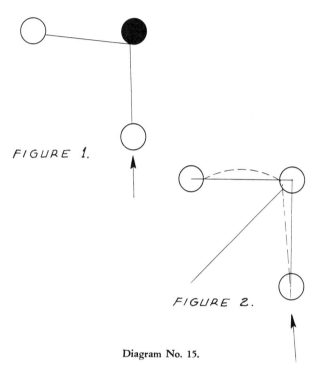

Diagram No. 15.

To make the draw as shown in Shot No. 1 on Diagram No. 16, strike the cue ball very low, without english; the cue ball hits the first object ball — a point, or hair's breadth, to the right of center. Another way to arrive at this dividing contact point is to first aim the cue ball full at the first object ball, and then switch the aim as little as possible toward the second object ball.

A little study and practice will make the ordinary draw very easy to master. Long draws, when the first object ball is a considerable distance from the cue ball, are not advised, as a one, two or three-cushion carom is preferable — and more certain.

Shots two, three and four in Diagram No. 16 are "spread" draws. To make the draw, as in Shot No. 2, when the balls are exactly at right angles, the cue ball is struck slightly below center, no english, and the inner or left edge of the cue is in alignment with the edge of the first object ball, as per diagram, thus hitting the first object ball one-quarter full.

To make the spread-draw, as in Shot No. 3, where the balls are at a sharper or a more acute angle than the right angle, the cue ball is struck below center and the exact middle of the cue tip is aimed at the edge of the first object ball, thus showing one-half the tip outside the edge, and hitting the first object ball one-half full.

To make the spread-draw (Shot No. 4), where the object balls are at an angle of 45 degrees from the cue ball, the cue ball is struck below center, without english, and the outer, or right edge of the cue tip is aimed in alignment with the edge of the first object ball.

On all these shots, when the cue ball is more than

12 inches from the first object ball, the first object ball must be struck fuller (nearer the center) as draw action is lost in proportion to distance between the cue ball and first object ball.

Another theory for the ordinary draw (Shot No. 5), is to strike the first object ball at the point opposite the center of the space between the cue ball and the second object ball, as previously explained in Diagram No. 14.

Absolutely no english should be used for draw shots. Simply strike the cue ball with a quick, moderate stroke — not too hard.

For all draws that require any speed, your bridge should be about six inches at the beginning of a stroke and 12 or more inches after cue ball has been struck, to insure a proper stroke. That is, the cue follows through the cue ball after the ball is struck, thus acquiring speed with an easy stroke.

English is used in making a draw shot only when it is necessary to throw the first object ball for "position." To throw the first object ball to the right, left or opposite english is used, and vice versa.

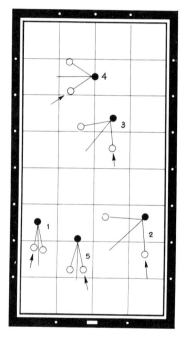

Diagram No. 16.

DON'T FAIL TO FOLLOW-THROUGH!

The experts continually give their attentions to this matter of stroke previously discussed, which is so important in creating draw action. The late George Sutton was one of a group of us on a train en route from New York to Chicago some time back. Sutton sat alone by a window, his right arm hanging at his side; the forearm in pendulum position and the wrist swinging gently.

He sat there, swinging his right wrist, for almost the entire trip. Just before arriving in Chicago he jumped up and called to me, "I've got it, Bill, I've got it."

"Got what?" I asked, somewhat startled.

"My stroke!" happily replied George.

PARTING DRAW SHOT ADVICE

Do not fear the draw shot. Use it whenever necessary without hesitation. Strict application of instructions and practice eliminate all danger of miscueing and jumping your cue ball. TRY TO JUMP THE CUE BALL SOMETIME—YOU WILL HAVE A HARD TIME DOING IT!

ONE-CUSHION OR CUSHION-CAROMS

Cushion Caroms, in which I hold the world title at present, brings into play all the attributes of straight-rail, balkline, and 3-cushions. It is a game requiring the utmost in execution; the skill and finesse of the straight-rail nurse, the long drive for position of balkline; and problems of angles in 3-cushions. In fact, it brings into play every conceivable shot in billiards.

The secret, or rather, the first and most important fundamental, of one-cushion shots — or cushion caroms — is bisecting the angle, and making an accurate carom. Knowledge of how to divide an angle and then expertly carom from an object ball to a cushion or from a cushion to an object ball is the basic principle of cushion-caroms. And it will considerably improve your game.

Bisecting angles is vividly shown in Diagram No. 17 In the shot at the right we find the two object balls in the center of the table, two diamonds away from each other and directly opposite the diamonds. Therefore, the point of contact on the cushion is the diamond between them. If you cue your ball in the center with *very* slight favoring to follow action, inasmuch as you want the cue ball to go in a natural forward motion, you must make the shot if you strike the diamond between the two object balls.

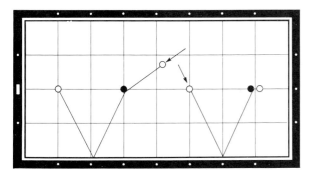

Diagram No. 17.

The object ball should be hit one-fourth to the left on this shot and here is where your ability to make caroms comes in. The reason you hit the cushion slightly closer to the first object ball than the objective diamond is to allow for the very little forward spin of your cue ball to equalize this difference. More on why you hit at the diamond in this way is explained in "Through and At Diamonds" section in following "Diamond System" chapters.

The shot on the left in Diagram No. 17 is the same shot except for it being a bank. You hit the cushion first at the bisecting point between the object balls and the cue ball — cue ball very slightly above direct center — to perfectly make this cushion-carom or one-cushion bank shot.

Of course, it is readily understood that the method of the bisecting point between the two objects or the dividing spot between cue and object ball on a bank only holds true when the object balls are on an imaginary line parallel to the cushion—as per Diagrams No. 17 and 18, Figure 1.

When the balls are not an equal distance from the

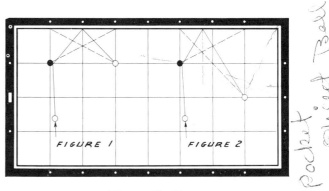

Diagram No. 18.

cushion, the point of contact on the cushion varies one way or the other according to the difference in distance they are away from the cushion.

Closely refer to diagram when reading following explanation: The only rule when object balls are at unequal distances from the cushion is: When one object ball is closer to the cushion than the other, strike the cushion at a point nearer to the closer object ball than the bisecting spot between the two object balls.

Perhaps Diagram No. 18 better illustrates the contact points on the cushion when the object balls are both at equal and unequal distances from the cushion.

Figure 1 in this diagram shows the object balls at equal distances from the cushion; therefore, hit the cushion at the bisecting point between them.

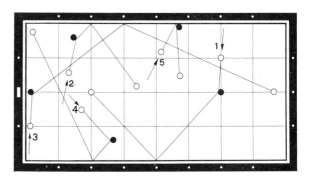

Diagram No. 19.

Figure 2 shows the object balls at unequal distances from the cushion with the first object ball closer to the cushion; therefore, hit the cushion at a point closer to the first object ball than the dividing spot between the two object balls.

The rule is: (Watch diagram closely) Draw imaginary lines (dotted in drawing) from each object ball to the spot on the cushion that the *other* object ball lies vertically opposite. Then the point on the cushion straight opposite the intersecting point of these imaginary (dotted) lines— also shown by a vertical dotted line in figure 2 in diagram —*ALWAYS* is the point on the cushion the cue ball *MUST* hit after contact with the first object ball, or before hitting an object ball in a bank shot.

To make the "cushion-carom" as per Shot No. 1 in Diagram No. 19, place the object balls on the "spots," and the cue ball between "spot" and opposite diamond. Then hit the first object ball one-half full with top ball, which means just slightly above the center. This should carry the cue ball to a point on the cushion in line with the middle diamond.

To make the cushion-carom shown in Shot No. 2, hit the first object ball half-full with no english or top ball.

If a shot is at an angle where the "middle point" is seen to be at a more obtuse or wider angle than 45°, as in Shot No. 3, hit the first object ball one-half full, with top ball, favoring right english rather hard to "spring" the cue ball to the third diamond on the long rail. It would be impossible to make a carom to the middle or fourth diamond, but hitting the third diamond with english, as per diagram, effects the same results as hitting the middle or objective point with no english. Be careful not to use a draw effect on any of these first three shots.

To make the No. 4 one-cushion carom on this diagram, hit the first object ball about one-third full, with a slight draw on the cue ball but without english, which should gather the balls. By not using english on this shot, the

"dead-ball" (See "Glossary of Terms") effect is obtained, thus holding the second object ball in the corner.

In the Shot No. 5 one-cushion carom hit the first object ball as thin as possible with top-ball, no english and just hard enough to "count" which will generally leave a good position and following easy shot.

The principal point to remember in cushion caroms is determining the objective point, which, of course, changes according to the position of the object balls, and not using english on most of the shots. Be careful not to use draw effect in playing any of the first three shots.

No exact rule is necessary for the use of english in cushion caroms. I repeat that practice soon will teach you the approximate amount of english necessary. If the cue ball is to run to the right, use right english, and vice versa.

For most cushion-carom shots, be sure to strike the cue ball slightly above the center to avoid causing a draw effect. The draw is used for one-cushion caroms only when it is impossible to use the above-center ball, because striking the cue ball slightly above center is always easier to control when the balls are fairly close together.

TWO-CUSHION, OR CUSHION CAROMS

TO MAKE the "two-cushion carom," Shot No. 1 in Diagram No. 20, strike the first object ball half-full, with considerable right-side english above the center. This will send the cue ball into the corner, from which it will take a "V" course to the second object ball. You will notice that almost all two-cushion caroms take the same "V" course from the corner, and after the "V" action is firmly fixed in your mind, most two-cushion caroms can be made with comparative ease.

The cue ball comes off the second cushion at an angle of about 37° when the cue ball hits near a corner, as in Shot No. 1, or as per dotted line in Shot No. 2. The "V" is about a 37° angle. An easier way to figure two-cushion caroms is to first figure the course of the cue ball from the corner of the table, and then make allowances. For example: If the second object ball in Shot No. 1 was located as per dotted line in Shot No. 1, a parallel point on the second cushion is the objective point. The two-cushion carom is considered a difficult shot, but close study and practice of the above suggestion should enable you to become proficient.

To make the two-cushion carom as per Shot No. 2, strike the cue ball slightly below the center with left english and hit the first object ball thin (about one-quarter full). It is plainly seen, in this shot, that if the first object ball was hit so that the cue ball went into the near corner, the "V" course, as per dotted line, would be followed and the second object ball would be missed very decidedly, hence use the "V" course as a guide and make allowance as per diagram. The dotted line shows

the "V" course as it would occur in this shot if the cue ball struck the corner.

To make the two-cushion carom as shown in Shot No. 3, make a plain carom from the first object ball to the first diamond on the long rail; the same distance from the end rail as the second object ball. Notice that the

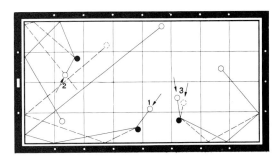

Diagram No. 20.

cue ball, after hitting the first rail, will hit the first diamond on the end (short) rail for the second cushion. A moderate stroke must be used to prevent the cue ball springing out of its true course. Don't use english. In case the balls are in a position so that the point on the first cushion cannot be reached by a plain carom, use english to get the same result, but the point you must hit on the cushion is slightly farther from the corner — as shown by dotted line.

STRAIGHT-RAIL

IF YOU practice and play straight-rail billiards first and continue to do so from time to time, you will be a much better 3-cushion and cushion-carom player.

Learn how to nurse the balls; in other words, how to play position with the balls close together and you will become proficient at playing any style of carom game. This is important knowledge to learn — the first requisite you must attain.

Straight-rail enables you to learn angles on the game that you'd never acquire unless you practiced this style of play.

Perhaps the reason straight-rail is not more generally played is the fact that most players, unless they are just starting to learn to play, have the false idea that it is too easy. Try to make a run of 50 points at straight-rail some time — and you'll find out how "easy" it is. You will, but with "reverse" english.

When you can make an occasional run of 100 at straight-rail, you can try the balkline game, but not before. Balkline is, in short, a more difficult style of straight-rail.

My recommendation to everyone, therefore, is: First play and become proficient at straight-rail before attempting 3-cushions, cushion-caroms or balkline.

The following 20 diagrams are the basic shots in straight-rail. Learn how to make them and you will have established a sound foundation as a shot-worker. The diagrams show the different positions to place the balls for practice — the positions you often will find them in when playing.

Follow the explanations accompanying these diagrams to the letter and practice one shot at a time until you become familiar with the way it should be played to make it, because they fully cover the fundamentals of straight-rail play.

In compiling these shots, it has been my aim to bring into play the fundamental shots which afford the greatest scope. I offer them to you with the sincere wish that they will be of invaluable assistance.

They will be just that, if you study them closely and consistently practice according to the instructions. All of them are known as "Gather" Shots, which means good position for the next shot. This is described by the circles on the diagrams. If the shots are correctly played, and made, all three balls should stop in the circles — giving you perfect next shot positions.

Remember: Straight-rail play is not too easy, but you can learn quickly, and when you do, you're on the road to being a better billiard player. It is advanced fundamental knowledge.

STRAIGHT-RAIL KEY SHOTS

(All Are "Gather"— Position — Shots)

Diagram No. 21—*Break Shot—Straight-Rail and Balk-line—Two-Cushion Shot*

Hold cue level.

Hit object ball ½ left.

Strike cue ball slightly above center.

Use 6-inch bridge.

Employ moderate stroke.

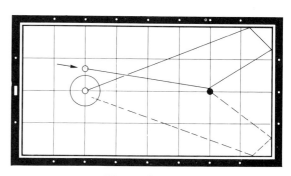

Diagram No. 21.

Diagram No. 22—*Rail Nurse*

Slightly elevate butt of cue.

Hit object ball ½ right.

Strike cue ball center.

Use 4-inch bridge.

Employ light stroke.

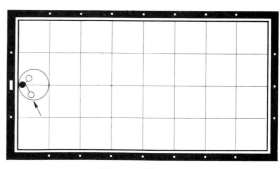

Diagram No. 22.

Diagram No. 23—*One or Two-Cushion Shot*

    Hold cue level.

    Hit object ball ½ left.

    Strike cue ball center.

    Use 5-inch bridge.

    Employ moderate stroke.

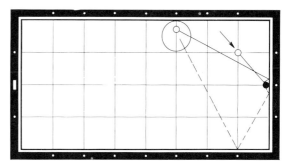

Diagram No. 23.

Diagram No. 24—*Bank Shot*

    Hold cue level.

    Hit cushion as per diagram.

    Strike cue ball center.

    Use 4-inch bridge.

    Employ light stroke.

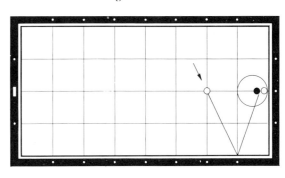

Diagram No. 24.

Diagram No. 25—*Draw Shot*

    Slightly elevate butt of cue.

    Hit object ball full, slightly left.

    Strike cue ball ½ below center, english left.

    Use 6 inch bridge.

    Employ moderate stroke.

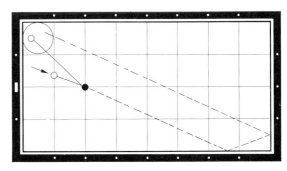

Diagram No. 25.

Diagram No. 26—*One or Two Cushion Shot*

    Hold cue level.

    Hit object ball ⅘ left.

    Strike cue ball slightly below center, english left.

    Use 6 inch bridge.

    Employ moderate stroke.

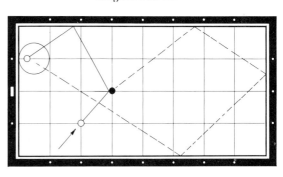

Diagram No. 26.

Diagram No. 27—*One or Two Cushion Shot*

    Hold cue level.

    Hit object ball ½ right.

    Strike cue ball ½ above center, english left.

    Use 6 inch bridge.

    Employ moderate stroke.

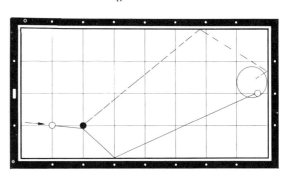

Diagram No. 27.

Diagram No. 28—*Bank Shot*

> Hold cue level.
>
> Hit cushion as per diagram.
>
> Strike cue ball above center, english right.
>
> Use 6 inch bridge.
>
> Employ moderate stroke.

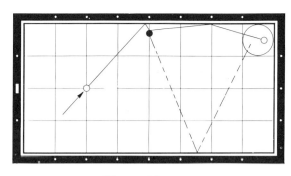

Diagram No. 28.

Diagram No. 29—*Two or Three Cushion Shot*

> Hold cue level.
>
> Hit object ball ⅓ left.
>
> Strike cue ball center, english right.
>
> Use 6 inch bridge.
>
> Employ moderate stroke.

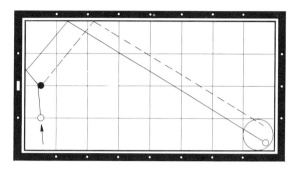

Diagram No. 29.

Diagram No. 30—*Follow Shot*

> Hold cue level.
>
> Hit object ball ⅘ left.
>
> Strike cue ball ½ above center.
>
> Use 6 inch bridge.
>
> Employ moderate stroke.

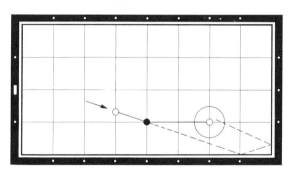

Diagram No. 30.

Diagram No. 31—*Kiss Shot*

> Slightly elevate butt of cue.
>
> Hit object ball ⅘ right.
>
> Strike cue ball slightly below center, english right.
>
> Use 6 inch bridge.
>
> Employ moderate stroke.

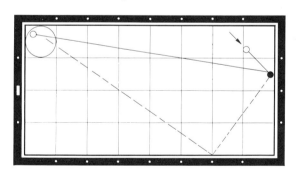

Diagram No. 31.

Diagram No. 32—*Two or Three Cushion Shot*

> Hold cue level.
>
> Hit object ball ½ right.
>
> Strike cue ball ½ above center, slightly english right.
>
> Use 7 inch bridge.
>
> Employ moderate stroke.

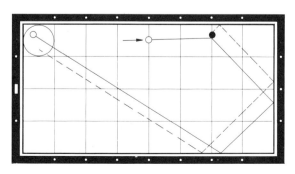

Diagram No. 32.

44

Diagram No. 33—*Dead Ball Shot*

      Slightly elevate butt of cue.

      Hit object ball ⅘ right.

      Strike cue ball slightly below center, english right.

      Use 6 inch bridge.

      Employ moderate stroke.

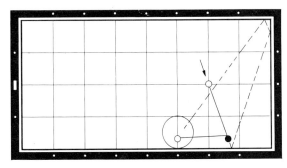

Diagram No. 33.

Diagram No. 34—*Two or Three Cushion Shot*

      Hold cue level.

      Hit object ball ¼ right.

      Strike cue ball center, english left.

      Use 6 inch bridge.

      Employ moderate stroke.

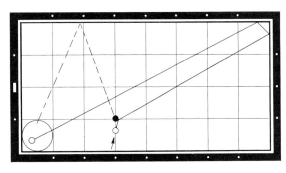

Diagram No. 34.

Diagram No. 35—*One or Two Cushion Shot*

      Hold cue level.

      Hit object ball ½ right.

      Strike cue ball center, slightly english right.

      Use 6 inch bridge.

      Employ moderate stroke.

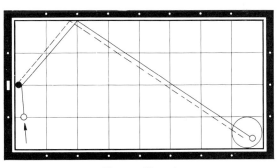

Diagram No. 35.

Diagram No. 36—*Three or Four Cushion Shot*

      Hold cue level.

      Hit object ball ⅓ left.

      Strike cue ball center, english right.

      Use 7 inch bridge.

      Employ moderate stroke.

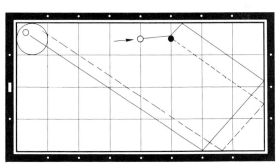

Diagram No. 36.

Diagram No. 37—*Draw Shot*

      Hold cue level.

      Hit object ball ⅘ right.

      Strike cue ball ½ below center.

      Use 5 inch bridge.

      Employ moderate stroke.

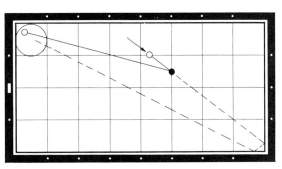

Diagram No. 37.

Diagram No. 38—*Dead Ball Draw*

    Slightly elevate butt of cue.

    Hit object ball ⅘ left.

    Strike cue ball slightly below center, english left.

    Use 5 inch bridge.

    Employ moderate stroke.

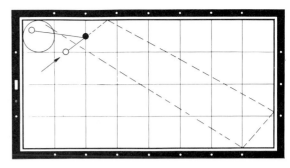

Diagram No. 38.

Diagram No. 39—*One Cushion Shot*

    Hold cue level.

    Hit object ball ½ left.

    Strike cue ball ½ above center.

    Use 5 inch bridge.

    Employ moderate stroke.

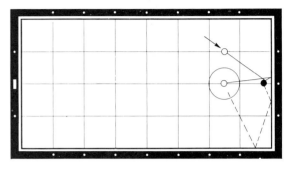

Diagram No. 39.

Diagram No. 40—*Cushion Follow*

    Hold cue level.

    Hit object ball full.

    Strike cue ball ½ above center.

    Use 7 inch bridge.

    Employ hard stroke.

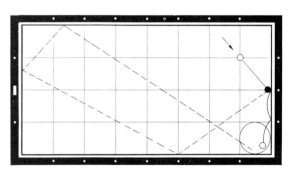

Diagram No. 40.

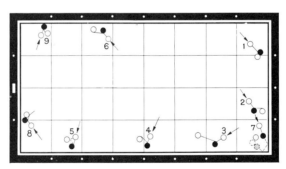

Diagram No. 41.

STRAIGHT-RAIL NURSE

If you will study the following shots and diligently practice according to instructions, you will be surprised how quickly you will learn the rail nurse, so important in straight-rail play. Knowledge of this phase of billiards will go far towards improving your game.

To learn straight-rail, or nursing the balls along the cushions, first place the balls in the exact position of Shot No. 1 in Diagram No. 41, one inch from cushion. Notice that the object balls are 45° from the cushion, which is the position in which they should always be kept. Aim the cue ball for the crotch, or center, of the two object balls; striking the cue ball very low without english. Striking above center gives speed to the balls, while striking below center has the opposite effect.

To make Shot No. 2 strike the white ball as per diagram with a low ball and right english. Use right english to work the white ball to the left. Right english on the cue ball will have the opposite effect on the first object ball. If directions are followed, the balls again should be in perfect position of 45° from the cushion.

To make Shot No. 3 hit the first object ball as per diagram with follow and left english. This should bring the balls to correct position. The follow is used to carry

46

the balls along, and the left english is used to carry the red ball along the rail. All straight-rail shots should be played with the wrist only, to insure a delicate stroke. Use right-hand or outside english to keep the object balls nearer the cushion.

To make Shot No. 4, hit the first object ball as per diagram with a low ball and left english, to carry the balls to the right. Be sure to hit the red ball full enough to carry it along. These directions soon will become clear by practice. The shots are easy; the stroke being the only difficulty, and that soon can be mastered if the wrist stroke striking the cue ball low is strictly followed.

To make Shot No. 5, hit the first object ball as per diagram; extremely thin, to prevent the balls "lining up." Strike your cue ball low, without english. Remember the correct position of the object balls is 45° from the cushion, as in Shot No. 1, and the balls should be played for that position at all times.

In Shot No. 6, hit the first object ball half-full with follow, left english, as per diagram, to bring the first object ball a little off the cushion to prevent the balls lining up. However, be sure to leave the second object ball near the cushion so that the 45° position can be obtained.

All the other straight-rail shots are variations of the foregoing shots, except the "masse," which is explained on following pages. Remember that right english on the cue ball has the opposite effect on the first object ball, and vice versa. Notice where the cue strikes the cue ball and the english used in these shots.

Shot No. 7 to "turn-the-corner," use left english and strike first object ball nearly full to make it take a course as per dotted line. Have your cue ball just "count" or "drop" on second ball, which will bring all balls about the same position as Shot No. 7, the correct position for the rail nurse, or 45°.

Shot No. 8 is the widely-known "anchor nurse" and is played with a most delicate stroke; right english, kissing from the red ball, and just touching the white ball without moving it. The cue ball returns the same way, without moving the white ball and rather full on the red ball, which remains "frozen" to the rail.

Shot No. 9 is the correct position for the "chuck nurse." It is played by striking cue ball above center with a very delicate stroke, slight left english and just hard enough to count. The top ball keeps the red ball on the rail. The chuck nurse was employed by my friend Charlie Peterson when he compiled 20,000 points in one hour, 41 minutes, 8 seconds at Chicago in 1935, an average of 3.296 points per second.

Practice shots similar to those described, because you will not only learn how to make the billiard, but always leave the object balls in good position for the next shot.

Practice is what makes the experts proficient. The principal object of constant practice is to enable you to make any kind of shot.

The science of straight-rail, cushion-caroms and balkline is keeping the balls in position for an easy following shot. The experts plan their play ahead. That's why the game seems so simple when watching them in action.

Much of my success is due to the fact that I take particular care to do just this. It was the main factor in keeping me at the top of the balkline world for many years.

3-CUSHIONS

INTRODUCTION

THREE-CUSHIONS is the most popular and attractive of all billiard games. With a thorough knowledge of cue fundamentals, applied intelligently, any player can master 3-cushions by using simple formulas of arithmetic.

Strict attention to foregoing fundamentals and suggestions will give you a distinct advantage in play, since they are the "one and only" rules of instruction and form to follow. So, if you haven't attained a goot stroke, etc., and a thorough knowledge of straight-rail, you will have difficulty in executing angle shots and becoming a good 3-cushion player.

Before going into the mathematical phase of this style of game. I advise you to learn basic 3-cushion shots—natural shots—which cover most of the needed knowledge. These shots are the natural (See "Glossary of Terms") "key-shots" that come up in angle play.

Advanced mathematical 3-cushion play, known as the "Diamond System," is explicitly covered in following chapters. The "Diamond System" shouldn't be studied until you have mastered the following shots. The numbers marked around the table on these diagrams, under object and cue ball headings, are for Diamond System calculation—fully explained in following "Diamond System" Chapters. Disregard them for the present, but after studying the System, come back to play these shots again and then use these numbers.

These following 24 basic 3-cushion key-shots (described on 20 diagrams) have been compiled to teach you the fundamental shots for good 3-cushion performance. They will be a great aid to you in becoming an expert 3-cushion player, if you apply your talent. Govern your play with their help.

Aside from the serious trend for a moment, speaking of 3-cushions reminds me of an amusing episode.

On one of my numerous tours, I was booked for a sort of grand opening exhibition in a western town by a billiard room proprietor who was new to the business.

Upon arriving for my date. he hastily approached me and excitedly exclaimed, "Mr. Hoppe, I don't know what we're going to do. I've been worrying about your 3-cushion exhibition. I certainly hope you can play 4-cushions just as well as you play 3-cushions, as I haven't a 3-cushion table in the house—they all have four cushions."

(Photograph No. 31)—Correct Position for the Opening or Break Shot.

(Photograph No. 32)—The break shot as shown by Gjon Mili's repetitive flash camera. Reprinted by courtesy of Mr. Mili and the editors of *Life Magazine*, in which this photo first appeared.

THREE-CUSHION KEY-SHOTS

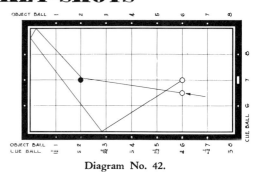

Diagram No. 42—*Break or Opening Shot*

    Hold cue level.

    Hit object ball ⅓ right.

    Strike cue ball center, slight english left.

    Use 7 inch bridge.

    Employ moderate stroke.

Diagram No. 42.

My position at the table, level cue, etc., for the opening or break shot is illustrated in Photograph No. 31. I always use the reverse of the shot shown in Diagram 42, starting on the right side and going to the left. The reverse means nothing—either side is satisfactory. Simply play the shot from the side you naturally prefer—your best side. For the shot diagramed, strike the cue ball at left-center, one cue tip to the left for left english and hit object ball one-third full. Practice this shot until you regularly can make it, because making or missing it often means the difference between victory and defeat. It is important that you know how to accurately score on this shot.

    An interesting study of the break shot actually being made by me is shown in Photograph No. 32. The plain ball is the cue ball, the ringed ball the first object ball, and the striped ball the second object ball. This photo appeared in LIFE MAGAZINE and is produced here through the courtesy both of their editors and Photographer Gjon Mili. This action is made possible only by Mr. Mili's repetitive flash camera which catches the entire course of the balls in the shot. Incidentally, this is the only camera of its kind in the world.

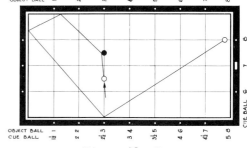

Diagram No. 43—*Natural, Three, Four, or Five Cushion Shot*

    Hold cue level.

    Hit object ball ⅓ left.

    Strike cue ball center, english left.

    Use 6 inch bridge.

    Employ moderate stroke.

Diagram No. 43.

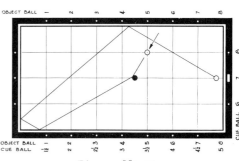

Diagram No. 44—*Three or Four Cushion Shot*

    Hold cue level.

    Hit object ball ¼ right.

    Strike cue ball center, slight english right.

    Use 6 inch bridge.

    Employ moderate stroke.

Diagram No. 44.

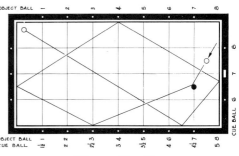

Diagram No. 45—*Five or Six Cushion Shot*

    Hold cue level.

    Hit object ball thin.

    Strike cue ball center, english right.

    Use 8 inch bridge.

    Employ hard stroke.

Diagram No. 45.

Diagram No. 46—*Rail First Three or Four Cushion Bank Shot*

    Hold cue level.

    Hit cushion as per diagram.

    Strike cue ball center, no english.

    Use 7 inch bridge.

    Employ moderate stroke.

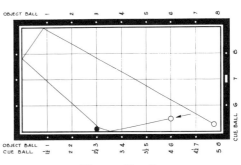

Diagram No. 46.

Diagram No. 47—*Four or Five Cushion Shot*

    Hold cue level.

    Hit object ball 1/4 left.

    Strike cue ball above center, english right.

    Use 7 inch bridge.

    Employ moderate stroke.

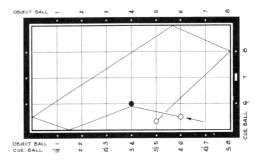

Diagram No. 47.

Diagram No. 48—*Five or Six Cushion Bank Shot*

    Hold cue level.

    Hit cushion as per diagram.

    Strike cue ball center, english left.

    Use 7 inch bridge.

    Employ moderate hard stroke.

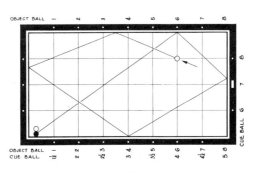

Diagram No. 48.

Diagram No. 49—*Four or Five Cushion Shot Off Frozen Ball On Rail*

    Slightly elevate butt of cue.

    Hit object ball 1/4 right.

    Strike cue ball below center, slight english right.

    Use 8 inch bridge.

    Employ moderate hard stroke.

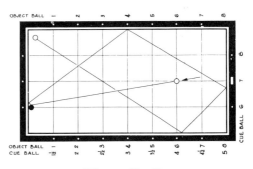

Diagram No. 49.

Diagram No. 50—*Running English Three Or Four Cushion "Dead-Ball" Shot*

    Hold cue level.

    Hit object ball 3/4 right.

    Strike cue ball center, english right.

    Use 7 inch bridge.

    Employ hard stroke.

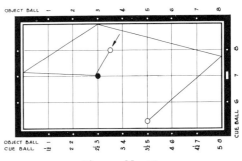

Diagram No. 50.

51

Diagram No. 51—*Extreme English Three or Four Cushion Shot*

    Hold cue level.

    Hit object ball ¼ left.

    Strike cue ball center, english right.

    Use 7 inch bridge.

    Employ moderate stroke.

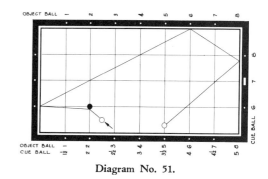

Diagram No. 51.

Diagram No. 52—*Plus System Three or Four Cushion Shot*

    Hold cue level.

    Hit object ball ¼ right.

    Strike cue ball center, english left.

    Use 6 inch bridge.

    Employ moderate stroke.

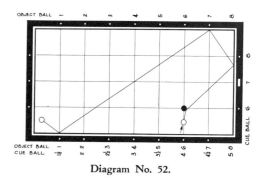

Diagram No. 52.

Diagram No. 53—*Three or Four Cushion Shot*

    Hold cue level.

    Hit object ball ¼ left.

    Strike cue ball center, english left.

    Use 6 inch bridge.

    Employ moderate stroke.

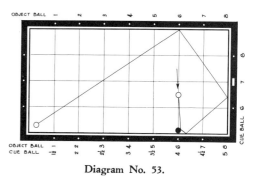

Diagram No. 53.

Diagram No. 54—*Reverse English on Fourth Cushion— Four or Five Cushion Shot*

    Hold cue level.

    Hit object ball ⅓ right.

    Strike cue ball below center, english right.

    Use 7 inch bridge.

    Employ moderate hard stroke.

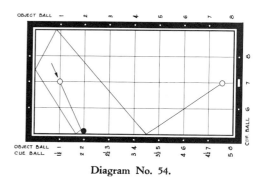

Diagram No. 54.

Diagram No. 55—*Four or Five Cushion Bank Shot*

    Hold cue level.

    Hit cushion as per diagram.

    Strike cue ball center, english left.

    Use 6 inch bridge.

    Employ moderate stroke.

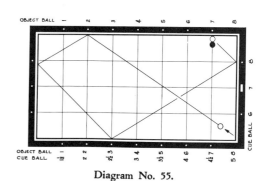

Diagram No. 55.

Diagram No. 56—*Three Cushion Double the Rail Shot*

   Hold cue level.

   Hit object ball ¾ right.

   Strike cue ball ½ above center, english
      right.

   Use 7 inch bridge.

   Employ moderate stroke.

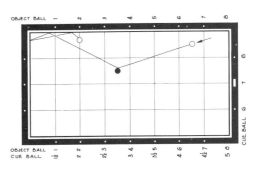

Diagram No. 56.

Diagram No. 57—*(Left)*—*Three or Four Cushion Reverse Bank Shot*

   Hold cue level.

   Hit cushion as per diagram.

   Strike cue ball above center, english
      left.

   Use 6 inch bridge.

   Employ moderate stroke.

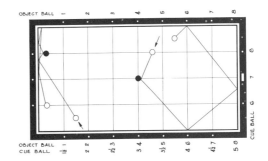

Diagram No. 57.

Diagram No. 57—*(Right)*—*Natural Short Angle Three Cushion Shot*

   Hold cue level.

   Hit object ball ¾ left.

   Strike cue ball center, english left.

   Use 6 inch bridge.

   Employ moderate stroke.

See above diagram

Diagram No. 58—*(Left)*—*Across-The-Table Three Cushion Cut Shot*

   Slightly elevate butt of cue.

   Hit object ball thin, left.

   Strike cue ball below center.

   Use 6 inch bridge.

   Employ moderate stroke.

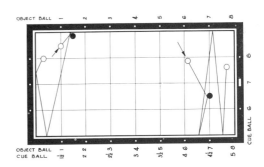

Diagram No. 58.

Diagram No. 58—*(Right)*—*Across-The-Table Twice Three or Four Cushion Shot*

   Slightly elevate butt of cue.

   Hit object ball thin, right.

   Strike cue ball center, slightly english
      left.

   Use 6 inch bridge.

   Employ moderate hard stroke.

See above diagram

Diagram No. 59—*Up And Down Table Three, Four, or Five Cushion Shot—No English Direction from First Object Ball*

Slightly elevate butt of cue.

Hit object ball ¼ right.

Strike cue ball slightly above center.

Use 8 inch bridge.

Employ hard stroke.

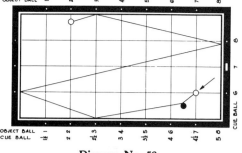

Diagram No. 59.

Diagram No. 60—(Left)—*Three Cushion Reverse Double-The-Rail Shot*

Hold cue level.

Hit object ball ⅔ right.

Strike cue ball slightly above center, english left.

Use 6 inch bridge.

Employ moderate stroke.

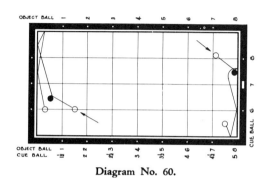

Diagram No. 60.

Diagram No. 60—(Right)—*Three or Four Cushions Follow Shot—Three Cushions on Two*

Hold cue level.

Hit object ball full.

Strike cue ball ½ above center, english right.

Use 7 inch bridge.

Employ hard stroke.

See above diagram

How this shot (Right, in Diagram No. 60) actually appears being executed by the repetitive flash lens is shown in Photograph No. 33, included here through the joint courtesy of *Life Magazine* and Photographer Gjon Mili. Note the *follow-through* of the cue.

Diagram No. 61—(Left)—*Double-The-Rail Top Spin Three or Four Cushion Shot—Three Cushions On Two*

Hold cue level.

Hit object ball ½ right.

Strike cue ball ½ above center, slightly english right.

Use 8 inch bridge.

Employ hard stroke.

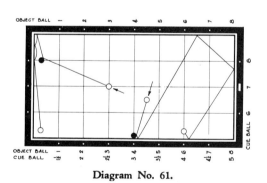

Diagram No. 61.

Diagram No. 61—(Right)—*"Around The Table The Wrong Way"—Running English Three or Four Cushion Reverse English Shot*

Hold cue level.

Hit object ball ¾ left.

Strike cue ball ½ below center, english right.

Use 7 inch bridge.

Employ hard stroke.

See above diagram

54

(Photograph No. 33)—The three-cushion on two shot, drawn on the right of Diagram No. 63, actually being made. Shown through the cooperation of both *Life Magazine* and Photographer Gjon Mili. Caught in motion by Mili's repetitive flash camera. Note the follow-through of the cue.

To make the three-cushion carom as shown in Shot No. 1 of Diagram No. 62, place the three balls in line, using the diamonds on the rails for measuring. Strike cue ball above the center with right english, hitting the first object ball one-third full. Be certain the cue ball strikes the right-hand long cushion near the third diamond. When the balls are anywhere near this position, all three in line, with second object ball on cushion, hit the first object ball on the left, as it is then made a "natural."

A natural is a term denoting a shot that should be easily made because of the perfect angles which can be obtained.

For example: If the first object ball in Shot No. 2 was three or more inches from the cushion, the proper procedure would be to hit the first object ball on the left side, then to the near cushion, then to the end cushion and, finally, to the other long cushion. This would make the shot easier than if played to the right of the first object ball. With few exceptions, all three-cushion shots should be made with natural running english, which means striking your cue ball slightly above center-right or left as is necessary.

Shot No. 2 is made with either two or four cushions. The first object ball is struck one-half full, hitting the right-hand long rail near the second diamond. Strike cue ball above center with right english. When the second object ball is near the corner, as in this shot the cue ball should always hit near the second diamond (right) cushion, but when the second object ball is 12 or 15 inches from the corner, as in Shot No. 1, the third diamond, marked X, is hit, etc. These "channels" should be learned, so when the second object ball is in this course, it is quickly

recognized. This is a very important point and should be remembered. (See "Corresponding Diamonds" in following "Diamond System" section.) The above applies to most three-cushion shots.

Shot No. 3 is made by striking the cushion first, then the first object ball, etc. Strike cue ball with right english, above center.

Shot No. 4 is known as the "snake shot" and is made with extreme "reverse english" (right in this case) and by striking your cue ball above center with a quick stroke.

Many three-cushion shots are missed because the cue ball is kissed off or interfered with by the object balls. In most cases, this can be prevented by driving the first object ball into the opposite corner, as per dotted line in Shot No. 1, and, if necessary, striking the cue ball a trifle lower than usual to offset the thinness with which the first object ball is struck.

For most three-cushion shots, the first object ball should be struck rather full. The diamonds can be used to great advantage in three-cushions. (See following "Diamond System" Chapters.) Especially the second diamond on the side rail, when the second object ball is in the corner on the opposite side. Look for a "big" ball; meaning a second object ball that is near a cushion, or near the corner. You then have two or more chances of counting—going in, coming out, directly on ball, off cushion, etc. See following "Science" Chapter.

Try to use just enough stroke to make the shots. In most cases, the easier you stroke, the more accuracy you will obtain. And always take the shortest shot; in other words, a short angle shot before a long angle one, which gives you less chance of a kiss, etc.

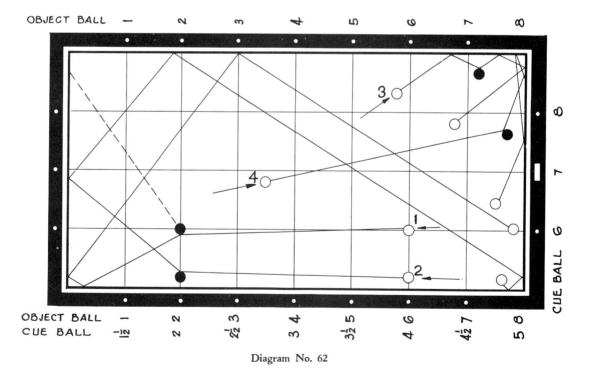

Diagram No. 62

MISUNDERSTOOD AND OFTEN-MISSED SHOTS

THIS is a good place to explain and illustrate shots that are often missed simply because they are misunderstood by the majority of players or haven't been correctly taught to them.

Take a look at the six cushion-first (often called rail-first) shots in Diagrams Nos. 63, 64, 65, 66 and 67.

On the right in Diagram No. 63 is a natural english cushion-first shot. On the left in this chart is a reverse english cushion-first shot.

In the natural english shot, you, of course, strike your cue ball at the center, one cue tip to the right—to obtain natural english in first striking the cushion, as you want the ball to hit the same cushion again after hitting the first object ball before going to the end cushion.

In the reverse english shot, you strike your cue ball at the center, one cue tip to the left—to obtain reverse english in first striking the cushion, because you want the ball to hit the end cushion after hitting the first object ball before coming back to the side cushion to count on the second object ball.

You again divide angles in this kind of shot. When the cue ball and first object ball are parallel with the side cushion—hit the cushion at the bisecting angle point exactly between them. See both shots in this diagram again for a clear picture of this.

If you do this, and cue the ball correctly, you must make the shot.

Diagram No. 64 shows the same kind of shot as the natural english one in Diagram No. 63, except that the cue ball is farther away from the cushion than the first object ball.

On bank-first shots in which the cue ball and the first object ball are at unequal distances from the rail, you find your point of contact with the cushion in the following manner: Find the midpoint as before. Measure along the rail *toward the nearer ball* a distance equal to the difference in distance from the cushion of the two balls. For example, if the *object ball* lies two inches *nearer the rail* than the cue ball, measure *from the midpoint* two inches along the rail *toward the object ball*. This is your point of contact for the shot. See Diagrams 64, 65, 66 and 67 showing the same shots as shown in Diagram 63 except that the balls are at unequal distances from the rail. In all these shots the point of contact with the cushion is found by the method just explained.

By playing these shots according to the foregoing methods, you must make them—all other requisites having been perfectly executed.

The shot shown in Diagram No. 68 is a short angle shot with the cue ball at the other end of the table from the two object balls. The shot is made by striking your cue ball in dead center, slightly favoring above center, and hitting object ball one-third to the right. This shot often is missed because english is used. The cue ball takes natural direction from contact with the first object ball.

The famous dead-ball shot with the cue ball at far end of the table is illustrated in Diagram No. 69. Regularly making this shot helped me win 20 straight games and the 1940 World 3-Cushion Championship. While appearing tough, the shot is easily made if correctly played. Strike cue ball *slightly* below dead center with level cue and hit object ball one-half to the right.

A reverse english bank is shown in Diagram No. 70. I played this as a feature shot in a recent Metro-Goldwyn-Mayer short. Being a reverse english shot, the cue ball is struck on the left side—center ball.

I am shown making this shot in Photograph No. 34. The tape on the table describes the path of the cue ball as per course drawn in Diagram No. 70.

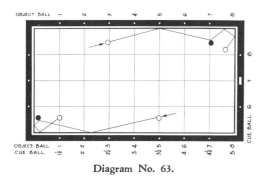

Diagram No. 63.

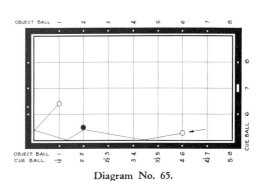

Diagram No. 65.

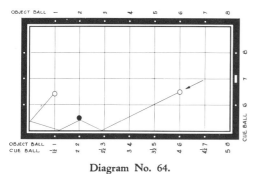

Diagram No. 64.

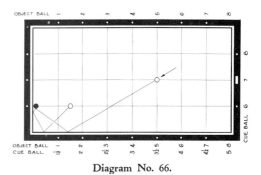

Diagram No. 66.

(Photograph No. 34)—Making the Reverse English 4-Cushion Bank. Hold cue level; Hit cushion as per diagram; Strike cue ball center, english left; Use 6 inch bridge; Employ moderate stroke.

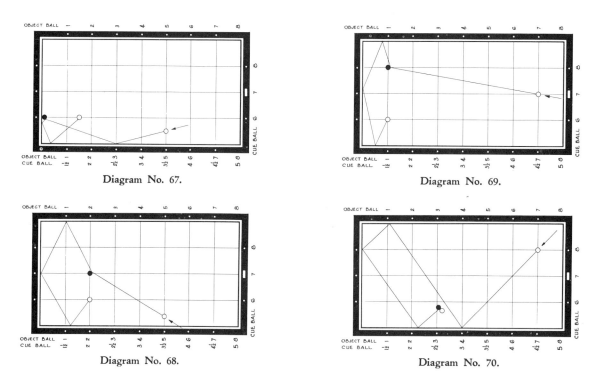

Diagram No. 67.

Diagram No. 69.

Diagram No. 68.

Diagram No. 70.

MASSE SHOTS

THE masse is the most difficult of all shots. It never should be attempted until you have become proficient at all other styles of play with a sound understanding and performance of fundamentals, especially the stroke. Beginners and masse shots do not mix. In short, the masse is the last phase of billiards to learn.

To make the ordinary masse, as Shot No. 1 in Diagram No. 71, hold the cue at an angle of 72°, or a little off the perpendicular. Strike the cue ball with extreme right english, back of the center. The best way to learn the exact spot to strike the cue ball is to rest the cue on the table, in alignment with the inner edges of the cue ball and first object ball, as in Shot No. 1; then raise the cue at exactly the same angle. This will bring it to

(Photograph No. 35)—Distance of bridge hand from cue ball and extreme upswing of stroke in free-hand masse.

the proper position, which is aiming at the "point of least resistance" or extreme edge of the first object ball. If the first object ball is not hit thin, it is impossible to hold the balls together, or get good position.

Never let the cue tip be partly outside the edge of the cue ball, as a miscue generally will be the result, and always hit back of the center, as shown in Shot No. 7. This drawing shows the proper place to strike the cue ball for all masse shots. The only chance for different shots is the elevation (slant) of the butt of the cue.

Ninety per cent of all masse shots are made with a cue elevation at an angle of approximately 78 degrees.

Do not strike the cue ball hard, because then it will not have time to curve. Do not use a slow stroke either. Neither is effective. It is necessary to use the wrist to get the proper snap effect for a masse.

To make the masse shown in Shot No. 2, play it the same as Shot No. 1, except that the cue is held more upright; the curve being sharper. In this case, the cue is held just off the perpendicular. The cue is never held absolutely perpendicular. Remember to give the cue ball a chance to curve properly by not striking too hard. Use a moderate, sharp, snappy stroke.

The cue should be held at an angle of 45° in Shot No. 3; making the shot a half draw and half masse. Strike the cue ball with no english and back of the center, as per sketch but not low. Use a quick, but not too hard stroke.

In the masse illustrated in Shot No. 4, when the cue ball is "frozen" or touching one of the object balls, the cue ball must first hit the free ball, as per diagram. Use right english, the least bit back of center.

Hold the cue almost upright and hit left side of first object ball.

The cue should be grasped in the right hand by forefinger and thumb for all masse shots. See proper grip for masse shots, Photograph No. 21 in "Making The Various Bridges" Chapter.

The masse shown in Shot No. 5 is uncertain and difficult. The only way it can be made is to shoot a little away from the direct line between the cue ball and the first object ball, and allow for the curve, about two inches from the edge of the first object ball when the cue ball starts eight or nine inches from the first object ball. Stroke according to the direction of cue in the diagram.

Shot No. 6 is made the same as Shot No. 5.

Learn to favor the side you want the cue ball to go to on all masse shots.

In Shot No. 7 I show the exact place to strike the cue ball for masses. Imagine a line from the near edge of the cue ball to the near edge of the first object ball. Then get a line through the cue ball at right angles to this line, as per diagram. Next, divide the ball into quarters, as per diagram, which will leave the quarter of the cue ball where the cue should strike. Notice that the cue strikes the cue ball just slightly below and to the right of center, for the shot diagrammed.

Shot No. 8, where the object balls are "frozen," and all three balls are in line, is difficult. It is made by shooting away from the object balls, returning in a sharp curve. Right english is used, and cue just off the perpendicular. Note direction of cue. The "free-hand" masse should be used in making this kind of shot.

The free-hand masse means that the bridge hand does not touch the table. See Photograph No. 22 again in "Making The Various Bridges" Chapter. Then study

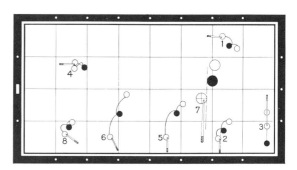

Diagram No. 71

Photograph No. 35. Notice that the bridge hand is approximately eight inches from the cue ball. This photo shows the cue at its extreme upswing. The arm—pressed against the side of the body—and the bridge hand are vertical to the body and horizontal to the table; coinciding with the level cue requirement in making customary shots.

It is important that you regulate the elevation of the cue by the distance you want the cue ball to travel. The further you want the cue ball to travel, the less you elevate the butt of the cue—increasing the force, or speed, of your stroke at the same time.

Remember, become proficient at all other phases of the game before attempting the art of making masse shots.

DIFFICULT SHOTS

HERE are seven difficult shots that often come up in play. They should be understood. However, don't attempt their execution until you have become an advanced player. Moreover, some of them are merely fancy shots.

To make the difficult close draw, Shot No. 1 in Diagram No. 72, when the cue ball is only one-quarter inch from the first object ball, strike the cue ball one cue tip below direct center and let the cue follow-through with a quick, hard stroke.

To make the force-follow, as per Shot No. 2, with the cue ball one-quarter inch from first object ball, strike the cue ball with right-follow english and also follow-through with a quick, hard stroke.

To make the kiss-masse, illustrated in Shot No. 3, use left english, just back of the center, hitting first object ball full. The extreme twist given by the english will force the first object ball out from cushion sufficiently to leave room for the direct return of the second object ball to cue ball, as per dotted line.

To make the force-masse, shown in Shot No. 4, aim the cue direct for second object ball, without english, and hold the cue at the slant shown in diagram, almost 90 degrees, which forces the cue ball to the second object ball. The first object ball takes a course to the left.

To make the kiss-follow, as shown in Shot No. 5, hit first object ball full, left-follow english, which causes the cue ball to "hug" the cushion and meet second object ball on its return from end cushion, as per dotted line.

Shot No. 6 is the kiss-masse. Use left english, slant cue about 45 degrees, meeting white ball in corner as illustrated.

To make the kiss-shot shown in Shot No. 7, strike cue ball with left english, slightly above center, meeting white ball in corner. This is a trick shot. Placing the balls properly as illustrated is half the secret of this shot, as it is in most fancy shots.

Shot No. 8 is the spin-shot, also a fancy shot. It is made exactly the same way as the first-close-draw-shot, except the cue ball must be hit slightly higher. Place balls one-quarter of an inch apart. The cue ball stops in the exact spot where the object ball rested and spins like a top.

Speaking of trick shots brings to memory an amusing incident that took place last spring on the Pacific Coast.

After my regular exhibition at a certain club, I announced that I would demonstrate about an even dozen fancy masse shots.

The manager of the club room hurried over to me and excitedly but politely and apologetically advised, "I'm sorry, Mr. Hoppe, but I'm afraid you'll have to confine your trick masse shots to ten. You see, there are only ten tables in the room."

I was confused for a moment, not knowing what he meant. Then a club member whispered enlightenment in my ear.

The last "expert" appearing there had put a neat 12-inch two-way rip in a good cloth, "making" his "lone" trick masse shot.

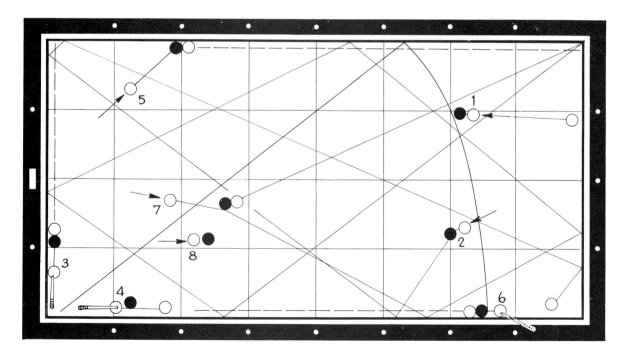

Diagram No. 72.

SCIENCE OF THE GAME

IT IS my purpose, in this chapter, to point out the application of the main science of billiards to the art of playing. It should be understood before taking up the following "Diamond System" instructions.

For instance, why is the path of the object ball always straight and that of the cue ball often curved? Why should the discussion of the effect of playing with or against the nap of the cloth be so important? Why is a shot made easier when the second object ball lies near a cushion?

I hope you might find some suggestions of interest and, possibly, of value in the following facts.

WHY ENGLISH CURVES THE PATH OF THE BALL

The curve of the path of a ball with english is caused by the friction between the small circle on which it is spinning and the cloth. The spinning ball, because of its shape and its pressure on the soft cloth, is sliding on a small circular surface; and the reason for the curvature under these circumstances is that in contact with the cloth the advancing side encounters more friction than the side which is moving opposite to the direction of the ball's progress, therefore, the former is somewhat retarded. The result is that the ball necessarily turns in this direction.

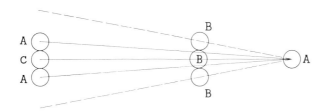

Diagram No. 73.

EFFECT OF THE NAP

On many tables a different curve when playing with and against the nap is noticeable. There is a little more friction going against the nap, but this should only occasion a slightly greater curvature in the same direction as when the ball is traveling with the nap.

"LONG" AND "SHORT" ROLLS

"Short" rolls, in strict billiard vernacular, mean when the cue ball runs or curves in, towards the long rail, because of the nap of the cloth.

"Long" rolls, in strict billiard vernacular, mean when the cue ball runs, or slightly curves away, from the long rail.

The nap of the cloth runs toward the foot of the table. Short rolls are evident with the cue ball going toward the foot of the table and long rolls often prevail when the cue ball is rolling toward the head of the table. The head of the table is that end where the name plate (trademark) appears imbedded on the rail.

Therefore, you can understand the often-heard expressions, "Playing the shot long" and "Playing the shot short;" meaning that a player intended coming off either the end (short) or side (long) rail, respectively, onto the second object ball. Or directly on the second object ball without aid of another cushion, by making the cue ball run either toward or away from the long (side) rail—short and long, respectively.

SIZE OF THE TARGET

The target presented by an object ball is very nearly twice the diameter of the ball, as seen by reference to Diagram No. 73. A ball at A aimed at the ball C will hit it if its path lies anywhere between AA' and AA'' as these lines pass the edge of C at a distance of half the diameter of the ball. The angular width of the target varies, of course, with the distance, and is greater in very nearly the proportion that the distance is less. A ball in the direction AB' or AB'' would graze B, but go quite wide of C at three times the distance. At a distance of nine feet, AC, the angle $A'AA''$ is about $2\frac{1}{2}$ degrees, and at one-third this distance, AB, the angular width of the target, $B'AB''$ is about $7\frac{1}{2}$ degrees. When a ball lies so near a cushion that the cue ball cannot pass behind it after touching the cushion, the target is practically much larger; and it is the largest possible when the object ball is in this position in a corner of the table.

On some shots, the second object ball is more than seven inches wide when it is in a corner. Say it is equidistant from the cushions, a little more than the width of the ball from each rail. The ball, of course, is 2 25/64 inches in diameter.

The cue ball, let's say, has struck the first object ball and completed the three cushions contact necessary for the point before it approaches the second object ball. It can strike the second object ball going into the corner or coming out. So you have the width of the second object ball plus twice the width of the cue ball to figure on. (This type of shot is known, in billiard vernacular, as a "big ball" shot.) Three times 2 25/64 inches is 7 11/64 inches, which is a comfortable leeway.

How true it is that you don't have that much leeway on all shots. On delicate shots you cannot allow a hairline margin of error.

STRIKING CUE BALL BELOW CENTER ON LONG SHOTS

In straight-rail or balkline when the object balls are far away from the cue ball — known as a long shot — strike the cue ball slightly below center with a quick and sharp, but not too hard stroke. By doing this you obtain more accuracy — preventing the cue ball from rolling off by striking it fairly hard and gaining perfect control over the object balls.

This type of shot is the same as the chip shot in golf.

In other words, this is the way to play the much discussed follow shot by striking the cue ball below center. You will use this shot many times during a game in your advanced play.

You can strike the cue ball fairly hard. It naturally will run fast until it loses its backspin. Then it will slow up in resuming its natural forward motion.

If you employ a fast follow action in playing this type of shot, you'd have no control over the object balls (for position) and less accuracy with the cue ball upon contact.

Use just enough speed to reach the shot. Practice will give you this "feel." And only play a shot this way when your cue ball is a good distance away from an object ball or balls (two and one-half diamonds or more); never when a "close" shot presents itself. And remember not to shoot with too much extra force. Practice this shot with the balls at different distances and you will learn something of great value.

SLIDE

Slide, meaning that the cue ball slides (slips) along on the cloth until the nap forces it to take the correct action imparted — natural roll — is something merely to know, but not to worry about.

Slide is evident on all shots and can't be avoided. However, it is well to know that more slide prevails on hard strokes — the harder the stroke, the more slide. Moreover, slide is more prominent on a new cloth.

EXTREMITY OF ENGLISH

The extremity of english was discussed in the foregoing "Applying English" chapter. It is wise to remember this point before touching upon the "Diamond System."

By putting extreme english on the cue ball from the center of the table and hitting the center diamond on a short rail, the cue ball will come back to the center diamond on a long rail. This is the very limit — extreme — of english.

Use this fact as a guide in making your cue ball go from diamond to diamond when playing the system. However, extremities of all sorts should be avoided whenever possible. To know this is very helpful in playing the "Diamond System," which immediately follows.

SPEED OF STROKE AND BALL

Naturally, speed of stroke and control of balls has much to do with the action obtained on all shots, especially in imparting english and playing the "Diamond System." Therefore, my advice at this time is for you to again read the "Speed and Force" chapter and pay specific attention — and thoroughly understand — the explanations of lengthening and shortening angles by use of speed. Also the relation of angles, in reverse, by increasing or decreasing the speed of the cue ball.

When you again have reviewed this lesson, you now are ready for "Diamond System" instructions.

My explanation of the "Diamond System" is not a closet study, but was written, so to speak, on the billiard table, with the cue as well as the pen. Theory, in every instance, has been put to the proof of not only experimental demonstration, but also world tournament achievement, and observation has led to explanation.

Fortunately, without going into profound mathematical analysis, it is possible to give a simple and intelligible explanation of this widely-publicized and much sought-after system which will improve your 3-cushion play. This is what I have attempted to do.

The "diamond system" will improve your game through the elimination of guesswork. Study these lessons carefully and pay particular attention to the accompanying charts. By learning the "diamond system" you will turn defeat into victory.

To get accurate results you must use natural, running english, center ball with moderate stroke on *all* shots played with the SYSTEM.

WHY DIAMONDS ARE ON THE RAILS

The diamonds, little pearl inlaid spots, or diamonds, on the top of the table rails were not put there for ornaments, as some believe, to add to a table's decorative appearance. They are there strictly as a guide for players to determine the correct angles of the table.

A billiard table is twice as long as it is wide. There are 8 sections on the side rail and 4 on the lower rail. These positions are divided by diamonds, which, in the diamond system, have numbers — cue ball and object ball numbers.

The inside numbers on the left side rails are object ball numbers. (See Diagram No. 74.) The diamonds are numbered from 1 to 7 and the lower corner is 8. At the same diamonds, the cue ball numbers run $1\frac{1}{2}$, 2, $2\frac{1}{2}$, 3, $3\frac{1}{2}$, 4, $4\frac{1}{2}$ and 5 on the side rail (5 being the corner) and they continue as 6, 7 and 8 on the end lower rail at the diamonds.

Moreover, the object ball numbers on the right side rail at the diamonds are numbered from 1 to 7. Again look at diagram. The lower right hand corner is 2, the next diamond is 3, and diamond 4 is at the center. Then the object ball numberings from 4 to the left side rail double-up, because the table is half as wide as it is long; making points 5, 6 (at the diamond), 7, and 8 at the lower left corner.

LOCATING THE NUMBERS

The diamonds always retain these regular numbers, counting away from the first short rail which the cue ball will hit.

The first thing to do is to memorize these numbers. As said before, the object ball location numbers and the cue ball position numbers as shown in Diagram No. 74 are the way these numbers run when you are standing at the head of the table. If you then go around and stand at the foot of the table, the location of the numbers simply is reversed. *The low numbers always start at the opposite end of the table from where you are standing to shoot.*

Memorize these numbers by first standing at one end of the table and studying them. Now go around to the other end of the table and do the same thing. Then practice determining their location from the two sides of the

table, remembering that the positions of the cue and object ball numbers always are determined, according to Diagram No. 74, by the first short rail the cue ball will hit.

You must remember these diamond numberings or markings, for they are your entire guide in the diamond system. Study and memorize both object ball location and cue ball position numbers and the starting points they cover.

CONNECTING DIAMONDS

The first step in using the diamond system for calculating 3-cushion shots is to understand connecting diamonds. Connecting diamonds make it possible to determine to which diamond a ball will travel after it hits a given diamond on the opposite side of the table.

You can prove to yourself, by banking a ball around the table, that diamonds do connect, but to simplify matters, the diamond connections which you must memorize are listed:

Diamond No. 1 on the left side rail (see Diagram No. 74 again) connects with Diamond No. 7 across the table.

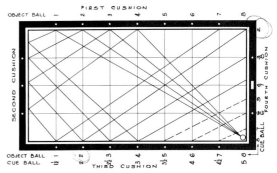

Diagram No. 74.

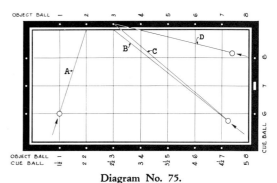

Diagram No. 75.

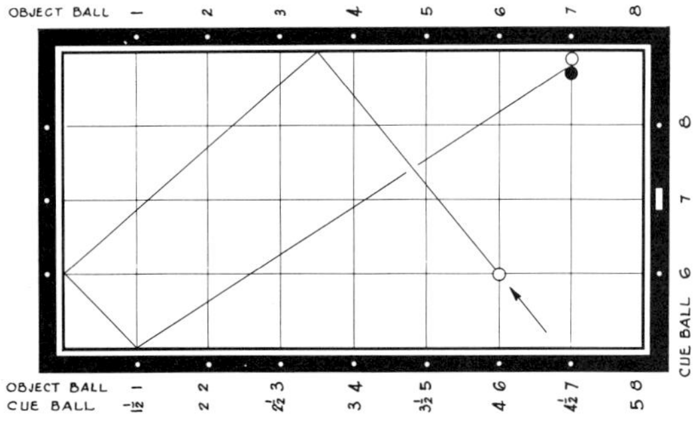

Diagram No. 76.

Diamond No. 2 connects with the far corner at the opposite side of the table.

Diamond No. 3 connects with Diamond No. 3 on the lower rail.

Diamond No. 4 connects with Diamond No. 4 (or the center diamond on the lower rail).

Diamond No. 5 connects with point "5" on the lower rail.

Diamond No. 6 connects with Diamond No. 6 on the lower rail.

Diamond No. 7 connects with point "7" on the lower rail.

Therefore, if object balls in a 3-cushion bank shot are at Diamond No. 7 on the right side rail, you know that you must carom the cue ball off the third cushion at Diamond No. 1 on the left side rail if the cue ball is to travel to the object balls, or Diamond No. 7 on the right rail. If the object balls are in the lower right hand corner, you know — because diamonds connect — that you must carom the cue ball off the third cushion at Diamond No. 2 to complete the point in the corner.

Connecting diamonds must be memorized, because the entire principle of the diamond system is based on where the cue ball strikes from one cushion to the other, on corresponding diamonds. Study the connections from one diamond to another with the utmost care. You must know where to come off the third cushion to make the billiard.

HITTING "THROUGH" (OR "AT") AND "OPPOSITE" DIAMONDS

Before going any further, I want to fully explain just where the cue ball should actually come in contact with the cushion when shooting for a given point. Most players always have been confused or misinformed, in determining angles, whether to shoot directly on a line to the spot on the top of the rail, or whether to shoot to the point on the cushion directly opposite this diamond. From now on, for clarity's sake, I will refer to this point of direction on top of the rail as the "diamond."

Diagram No. 75 fully explains where your cue ball should strike the cushion. In other words, you shoot "through" the diamond, as Shots "D" and "C" and NOT at a spot on the cushion directly opposite the diamond, as illustrated in Shot "B."

This rule always holds true when shooting from the end rails or from the corner. When shooting from the side or long rails, you hit the cushion at a point directly *opposite* the desired diamond, as shown by Shot "A" in Diagram No. 75.

Therefore, when playing from the end or short rails, or from a corner, shoot "through" (or "at") the diamonds; when playing from the side or long rails, shoot at a spot "opposite" the diamond.

You will notice, in Shot "D," that you actually hit the cushion at a point opposite Diamond No. 4, when shooting at the No. 3 Diamond.

Always shoot on a direct line to the diamond—either "through" or "opposite" as the case may be, governed by the point from which you're shooting—side or end rails.

NOTE: For clarity's sake, all the following Diamond System diagrams are drawn with the cue ball hitting the cushions opposite the diamonds.

BANK SHOTS

You know, by the use of connecting diamonds, that a ball banked around the table will travel from a given diamond on one side of the table to a certain diamond on the opposite side. For example, Diamond No. 2 on the left rail connects with the right corner on the lower rail. Diamond No. 1 on the left side rail connects with

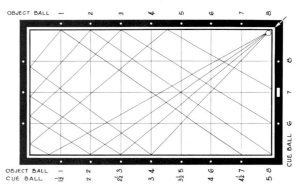

(Diagram No. 77)—Diamond (5) System; Marks on two long rails prove 5 diamonds and results of angles. Use natural, running english, center ball, with level cue and moderate stroke.

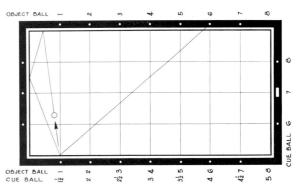

(Diagram No. 78)—Diamond (1½) System; Marks on two long rails prove 1½ diamonds and results of angles. Use natural, running english, center ball, with level cue and moderate stroke.

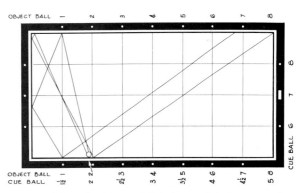

(Diagram No. 79)—Diamond (2) System; Marks on two long rails prove 2 diamonds and results of angles. Use natural, running english, center ball, with level cue and moderate stroke.

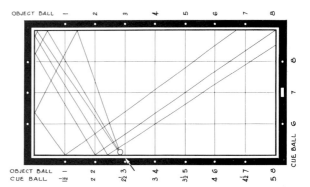

(Diagram No. 80)—Diamond 2½ System; Marks on two long rails prove 2½ diamonds and results of angles. Use natural, running english, center ball, with level cue and moderate stroke.

Diamond No. 7 on the right side of the table. (See Diagram No. 74 again.)

Knowing the diamond numbers and the connecting diamonds, you are now ready to play a simple 3-cushion bank shot by the diamond system. (See Diagram No. 76.) You find the object balls are on Diamond No. 7 on the right side of the table and you must hit three cushions with the cue ball before striking both object balls. Proceed first to play the shot backwards:

Finding the object balls at Diamond No. 7 on the right side of the table, you know that the connecting diamond on the left side is No. 1. Having determined this, you now consider the cue ball and find it lies in cue ball track 4½. Your next problem is to find to which point on the first (right side) cushion the ball must be driven to bring it back to the rail you are playing from at Diamond No. 1. Since the cue ball track is 4½ and the object ball number at that diamond is 1, you subtract 1 from 4½ and get 3½; learning that you must hit diamond 3½ on the opposite rail. A double check that you can use to be certain your figuring is mathematically perfect is to add the total of the object ball numbers on the two long, or side, rails. This total *MUST* always equal the original cue ball starting position number. The shot diagrammed shows the object ball numbers one and 3½, equaling 4½, the cue ball number.

In bank shots, the cue ball is the base of calculation, or object of your simple arithmetic. Calculating the shot, you must first determine the position of the object balls and find the connecting diamond across the table. Next, you find the cue ball track. Having found it, you subtract the object ball number at the connecting diamond (1) from the number of the cue ball track (4½) to find the point of contact (3½) on the first cushion.

You would play this shot in the same way if the object balls were any place on an imaginary line between Diamond No. 1 on left cushion connecting Diamond No. 7 on right cushion.

It is important to remember that the system is based on the principle that the total of the contact points (object ball numbers) on the two long rails will equal the number of the "starting point" (cue ball position number). For example, (see Diagram No. 77) Diamond (5) System. From the "starting point" (5) you will note, by following each angle, that the contact points of the lines on the two long rails will total 5 diamonds.

Fix this principle in your mind and the following method of calculating all angles will be easily mastered.

First figure the "location" of the object balls by marking the diamond or space between the diamonds on the *SECOND* long rail where your cue ball must strike in order to effect a count, then subtract the number representing the object ball "location" from the "starting point" number of your cue ball and the result will be the number of the diamond or space between the diamonds to strike on the *FIRST* long rail. To study this in actual practice, place your cue ball in the corner (5) and the object balls on the line of the angle extending from the third diamond on the second long rail; subtract the object ball "location" (3) from cue ball "starting point" (5), giving (2) as the diamond to strike on the first long rail. Use Diagram No. 77 for a guide while reading or practicing this instruction.

To see me doing a similar 3-cushion bank shot procedure in an actual reproduction, take a look at Photograph No. 36. Here I have placed my cue ball in the corner (5) and the object balls on the imaginary line of the angle extending from the second diamond on the second long rail. Subtracting the object ball "location" (2) from the cue ball "starting point" (5), gives me (3) as the diamond to hit on the first long cushion. The

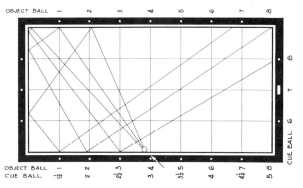

(Diagram No. 81)—Diamond (3) System; Marks on two long rails prove 3½ diamonds and results of angles. Use natural, running english, center ball, with level cue and moderate stroke.

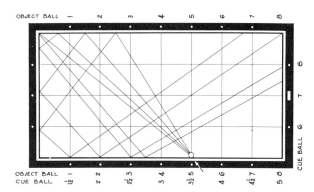

(Diagram No. 82)—Diamond (3½) System; Marks on two long rails prove 3½ diamonds and results of angles. Use natural, running english, center ball, with level cue and moderate stroke.

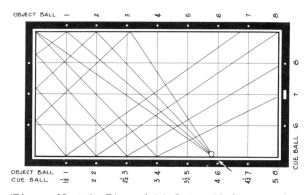

(Diagram No. 83)—Diamond (4) System; Marks on two long rails prove 4 diamonds and results of angles. Use natural, running english, center ball, with level cue and moderate stroke.

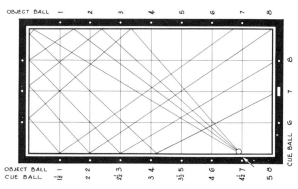

(Diagram No. 84)—Diamond (4½) System; Marks on two long rails prove 4½ diamonds and results of angles. Use natural, running english, center ball, with level cue and moderate stroke.

use of tape in the photo shows the course of the cue ball from cue ball position in corner (5) to Diamond No. 3 on first long rail, to end cushion, to Diamond No. 2 on second side (long) cushion, and then on to the object balls to count the billiard.

"Starting point" or "location" numbers can be given to any space or any part of the space between any of the diamonds. For instance, if the cue ball is placed exactly halfway between (4½) and (5), its "starting point" number would be (4¾). If the object balls were then placed on a line extending from the middle of the space between the third and fourth diamond on the *SECOND* long rail, the object ball "location" number would be (3½). 4¾ minus 3½ equals 1¼, or the exact place to strike on the *FIRST* long rail.

After you have carefully calculated the angle, concentrate your attention on hitting the *FIRST* long rail at the right place. Forget about the object balls. The angles will take care of themselves if you start your shot right.

The lines drawn on the accompanying diagrams — Nos. 77 to 88, inclusive — show the course the cue ball takes. Therefore, it will be plain to you that if the cue ball is placed at any point on the line drawn from the "starting point" to the first long rail, and the object balls at any point on the extension of the same line from the second long rail, the scoring of the point will be made certain by merely striking the right place on the first long rail. The same will be true of any imaginary line that you will draw, if correctly figured according to the method used in this system.

After you have become thoroughly familiar with the "starting point" numbers and the method of calculating the object ball "locations," carry your study and practice further by learning the results of angles which are shown on the diagrams by the lines drawn from the second long rail to the finishing points.

The diamond system is based on World's Championship playing conditions, on "1845" Cushions. Accurate results will be obtained by making allowances for varying conditions. You will quickly learn the correct allowances to be made by carefully observing the results of a few practice shots. Carefully practice shots of each of the 12 cue ball positions, shown on Diagrams Nos. 77-88. It is best to thoroughly learn one position of the system before studying the next cue ball position.

INSTINCT

In the following few lines, I will attempt to explain how you can play the diamond system by instinct or mathematical design. Many of the game's leading stars play by "instinct," but they know the mathematics of 3-cushion play. Perhaps it is more correct to say they play "mathematically by instinct."

Diagram No. 89 shows a simple 3-cushion shot. Any 3-cushion player knows that if he hits the first object ball on the left side with the cue ball that the cue ball will strike cushions one, two and three, and finally travel in the general direction of the second object ball, and, probably, complete the billiard point. A player knows that by instinct or just plain observation.

A trained 3-cushion player knows that, too, but he resorts to mathematics to rule out chance. (See Diagram No. 89 again.) He figures that the first object ball is the object of his calculation. He calculates, then, that his shot lies in cue ball track 4½. He knows that his cue ball must strike the third cushion at the No. 2 diamond in order to travel to the corner where the second object ball is resting.

Since his object ball lies in track 4½ and inasmuch as he must hit diamond No. 2 on the third cushion, he

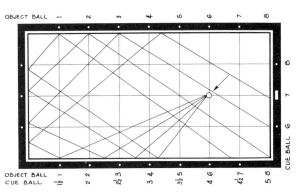

(Diagram No. 85)—Diamond (5½ "Spot") System; Marks on two long rails prove 5½ diamonds and results of angles. Use natural, running english, center ball, with level cue and moderate stroke.

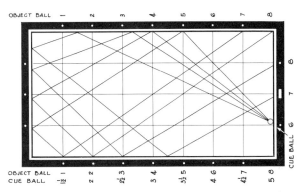

(Diagram No. 86)—Diamond (6) System; Marks on two long rails prove 6 diamonds and results of angles. Use natural, running english, center ball, with level cue and moderate stroke.

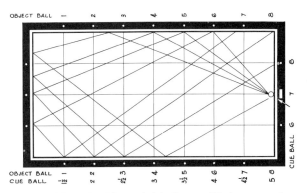

(Diagram No. 87)—Diamond (7) System; Marks on two long rails prove 7 diamonds and results of angles. Use natural, running english, center ball, with level cue and moderate stroke.

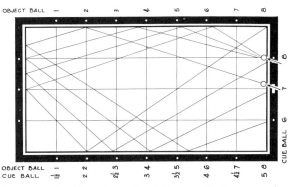

(Diagram No. 88)—Diamond (8) System; Marks on two long rails prove 8 diamonds and results of angles. Use natural, running english, center ball, with level cue and moderate stroke.

knows that his carom off the first object ball must strike the first cushion at the 2½ diamond, because 2½ from 4½ is 2, or the diamond he is seeking on the third cushion.

Moreover, to prove this, the total of the two diamonds he must hit on the long rails is 4½ (2½ plus 2) which equals cue ball track 4½.

If he plays the shot correctly, using these calculations — and *PROVIDING* his carom is executed right — he will make the point. Therefore, mathematics, or rather the diamond system, rules out chance in 3-cushion billiards.

OBJECT BALL SHOTS

When a 3-cushion shot requires that an object ball be hit first with the cue ball, the object ball instead of the cue ball, as in bank shots, is used as the basis of our calculations. (See Diagram No. 90.)

Studying this shot backwards, as you do all 3-cushion shots, you find that to bring the cue ball where the second object ball is resting, the cue ball must carom off the third cushion at Diamond No. 3, since this is the connecting diamond for which you are shooting.

You know that you must hit Diamond No. 3 on the third cushion. Now, going back to the first object ball, you determine that your course in cueing the ball lies in cue ball track 6. Since your object on the third cushion is 3 and your track is 6, 3 from 6 equals 3, or the diamond you must strike on the first cushion after you carom off the first object ball.

This shot would be accomplished under the same mathematical formula if the second object ball was any place on the table in the line between the two connecting Diamonds 3 — on the third and fourth cushions, respectively (see Diagram No. 74 again) — or if the first object ball was at any point on cue ball track 6.

You can now further see how important caroms are in 3-cushions. If you are unable to carom, as you plan, off the first object ball to Diamond 3 on the first cushion, you have no assurance that the shot will be completed as you play it. The smart 3-cushion player will constantly practice on caroms.

BREAK OR OPENING SHOT

The break, opening or "spot" shot in 3-cushions, finds the two object balls "spotted" as per diagram No. 42, and the cue ball placed within six inches and on a line or behind the object ball at the head of the table. (The head of the table is the end where the name plate appears. However, in strict billiard vernacular, the "head" of the table is always the end you're shooting from. The far end, therefore, is referred to as the foot. The two long cushions are designated as side rails.)

Studying this shot backwards, you find that the second object ball lies between object ball numbers 2 and 3. So you can figure the shot from object ball number 2½ — knowing the cue ball must come off the third cushion at this point.

Now, going to the first object ball, you find it lies in cue ball track 3. Inasmuch as you subtract the object ball number from the cue ball number to determine the diamond on the first cushion, you know that the diamond on the first cushion is ½, because 2½ (the object ball number) from 3 (the cue ball number) equals ½.

Therefore, to make the shot and count, you must carom the cue ball off the first object ball to Diamond ½ on the first cushion. The cue ball then will bound to the end rail and come back to the third cushion at Diamond 2½. Since the second object ball lies in object ball track 2½, you will make the billiard if the shot is correctly played.

As previously explained, the break shot is made by striking the cue ball with left side english, slightly above

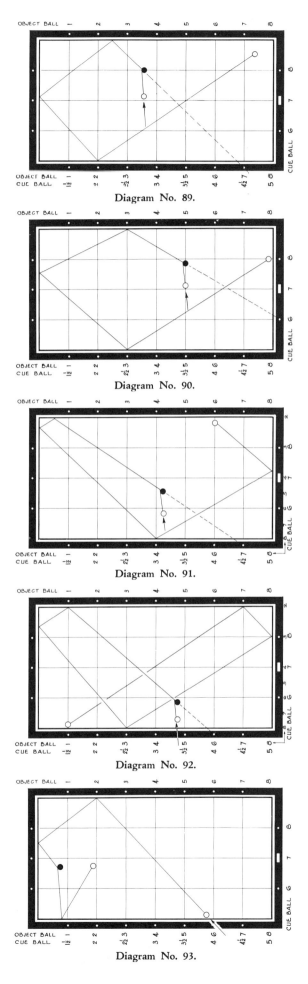

Diagram No. 89.

Diagram No. 90.

Diagram No. 91.

Diagram No. 92.

Diagram No. 93.

center, and hitting first object ball about 1/3 to right, as per diagram No. 45. If cue ball is placed on right side of second object ball, use right side english and hit first object ball the same — about 1/3 to left.

The opening, break or spot shot should make you further realize just how important caroms are in billiards. Unless you can carom the cue ball from the first object ball to the first cushion at imaginary "Diamond" No. 1/2, you'll never be a consistently good player. Practice caroms!

MORE ABOUT CONNECTING DIAMONDS

The shot illustrated in Diagram No. 91 can be made by mathematical deduction. With the exception of one series of lessons by my pal, Charlie Peterson, to date there has been nothing else written on 3-cushion instructions to guide a diamond system student in figuring it out.

I already have discussed the diamond system of 3-cushion play and the necessity of memorizing connecting diamonds. You know (see Diagram No. 74 again) that Diamond No. 1 on the left side of the table will connect with Diamond No. 7 on the right; that Diamond No. 2 on the left connects with the right corner on the lower rail; that left rail Diamond No. 3 connects with Diamond No. 3 on the lower rail, etc.

However, in the shot shown on Diagram No. 91, the second object ball is at the second diamond from the lower end (head) of the table on the right rail. If you could carom a ball from the right (first) cushion exactly into the upper left corner you might make the shot, but the chances are against you.

Therefore, you must learn now that diamonds connect all around the table. For example, Diamond No. 3 on the left rail connects with Diamond 3 on the lower rail, while the latter diamond connects with Diamond 7 on the right rail. Diamond No. 4 on the left rail connects with Diamond 4 on the lower rail, and the latter diamond connects with the second diamond on the right from the lower cushion or Diamond No. 6. (See Diagrams Nos. 74 and 91.)

Knowing this you can figure the above 3-cushion problem from the lower rail. You know you must come off Diamond No. 4 on the lower rail to connect with the second diamond from the lower end on the right rail. You know, too, that Diamond No. 4 on the lower rail connects with Diamond No. 4 on the left rail. Therefore, your object diamond on the left rail — or the third cushion — is No. 4.

Your cue ball position is 4½. Subtracting the object ball position (Diamond No. 4) from the cue ball position (4½), you learn your point on the first cushion is "Diamond" ½. A ball shot with the proper natural, running english to "Diamond" ½ will carry it around the table to count.

AROUND-THE-TABLE SHOTS

Diagram No. 92 illustrates a twice-around-the-table shot which will impress upon you the necessity of learning the diamond system and it will re-emphasize what you *must* know about connecting diamonds.

This diagrammed shot shows the first object ball on cue-ball track 4 and the second object ball in the upper left corner of the table. Studying this shot backwards, you know you must come off the right (first) cushion at Diamond No. 7 to come back to the approximate position of the second object ball in the upper left hand corner. You know that Diamond 7 connects with Diamond 3 on the lower rail and that Diamond 3 on the lower rail connects with Diamond 3 on the third (left) cushion.

Knowing these connecting diamonds, you are now ready to find your object diamond on the first (right-hand) cushion. You find the first object ball lies in cue ball track 4 (remember this is a carom shot). Your object diamond on the third cushion is No. 3. Therefore, Diamond No. 3 (our object) subtracted from 4 (our cue ball position) gives us 1 or Diamond No. 1 on the first (right) rail. An accurate carom, which will send the cue ball from the first object ball to the first cushion at Diamond No. 1, will send the cue ball around the table to the above mentioned connecting diamonds and complete the count.

Splendid practice can be obtained by moving the balls around; keeping the first object ball on cue ball track 4 and figuring your own five or six cushion shots. Simply remember your rule for subtraction and check by addition, as previously explained.

An around-the-table bank shot actually being made is shown in Photograph No. 37 by means of the repetitive flash camera, previously explained.

Here you see me shooting out of cue ball position No. 5. You know, by the connecting diamonds, that I must come off Diamond No. 3 on the lower rail, to go to the first diamond up from the corner on the left rail to make the shot, inasmuch as the object balls lie on an imaginary line between the connecting diamonds No. 1 on the right (side) rail and No. 7 on the left (side) rail.

Therefore, my object diamond on the third, fourth and fifth cushions is 3 and subtracting this number (3) from my cue ball position number (5), gives me Diamond No. 2 as the spot to hit on the first cushion. The photo shows me hitting this point ("Through" Diamond No. 2) on the first cushion and the accurate course of the cue ball to the end rail, then to Diamond No. 3 on the second long rail, and completing the connecting Diamond "3" course to make the shot.

So you now have been instructed and shown, and know how to make fundamental 3-cushion shots through the diamond system of play. Eighty per cent of 3-cushion shots can be made by use of this system.

FAMOUS "UMBRELLA" SHOT

The celebrated "umbrella" shot (see Glossary of Terms for explanation) is shown in Diagram No. 93. This shot can be played by use of the "Diamond System."

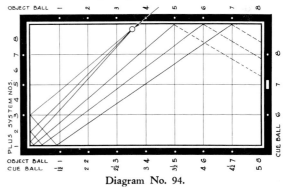

Diagram No. 94.

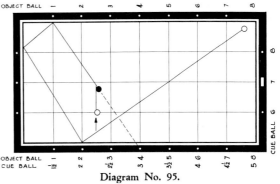

Diagram No. 95.

As the balls lie, we know that we must carom our cue ball off the edge of the red, or first object ball, to correctly hit the third cushion to make the billiard. So we line up the shot accordingly and find that by hitting the edge of this first ball — a continuation of this imaginary line would bring us to object ball location No. 2 on the third (left-side) cushion.

We also know our cue ball lies in cue ball track No. 4 in shooting to the first (right) side cushion. Therefore, 2 from 4 gives us the No. 2 diamond as the spot we must hit on the first cushion. Practice this shot with natural, running english, center ball, and you soon will grasp the stroke to employ and ability to regularly make it. Then practice other "umbrella" positions, using the above described calculations in playing them. However, umbrellas are tough shots — even for the experts — and shouldn't be attempted unless no other shot presents itself.

PLUS SYSTEM

The plus system, sometimes referred to as the "Plus 2 System," is illustrated in Diagram No. 94.

The numbers of the diamonds, and numbers between them, which serve as the basis of this specific system, are found on the upper (short) rail. The upper left-hand corner is 1, and reading to the right, the first diamond is 3, the second or middle diamond is 5, and the third or first diamond from the right-hand corner, is 7. Midway between these diamonds are numbers 2, 4, 6 and 8, respectively, because, once again, a table is twice as long as it is wide and we are dealing with a short rail, playing from a long (side) cushion.

The plus system is used in bank shots when the cue ball lies near a long, or side cushion, and the object balls are on, or near, any of the dotted lines shown on Diagram No. 94. Any place hit on the end rail with the cue ball will bring it back that exact distance, or number of diamonds — according to the end rail numberings explained above — further *down* the long rail from where the cue ball started or was shot from. (See Diagram to clearly get this explanation.)

Therefore, when playing from any diamond on the side rail to the upper (end) rail 1/2 diamond from the corner, the cue ball will return to the same side rail at a point two diamonds lower down on the cushion from the starting point of the cue ball. The reason — again — is that the cue ball, by hitting the end rail 1/2 diamond from the corner, actually hit plus system number 2 which brings it back two diamonds further down the side rail from where it started.

Natural english should be used.

To reach a point on the side rail only one diamond lower down the rail than the cue ball's starting point, the cue ball is shot directly into the corner.

To reach a point three diamonds further down the rail than the starting point of the cue ball, shoot the cue ball to Plus System Diamond No. 3 on the end rail — or one full diamond from the corner.

The dotted lines on the diagram show the track of the cue ball after leaving the side rail at Diamonds No. 5, 6 and 7 on its return; how it will come off Diamonds Nos. 5, 6 and 7, respectively, and continue to the lower end rail.

Naturally, object balls anywhere on these dotted lines will be hit if you correctly play the shot.

On Diagram No. 94, the cue ball starts at the No. 4 diamond on the right (side) cushion and returns to Diamonds Nos. 5, 6 and 7, respectively.

Of course, it is understood that you can parallel at any point and obtain the same result.

SUMMARY

In order to play expertly, you *must* know the diamond system, which enables you to quickly subtract the object ball position from the cue ball position to determine the object diamond on the first cushion. This is all you have to know for a natural angle 3-cushion shot. However, when the shot requires more than three cushions — say four or five — you must know the connecting diamonds on the other rails to be certain of the course of the cue ball around the table.

Diagram No. 95 will prove to you that a ball shot from cue ball track 3 to Diamond No. 1 on the far cushion will come back to object ball Diamond No. 2 on the third cushion and that Diamond No. 2 connects with the corner. This diagram shows that by subtracting the desired diamond (2) on the third cushion from your cue ball position — be it 4 or 8 — you will find the diamond on the first cushion which will bring the cue ball back to the third cushion at Diamond No. 2 and thence to the corner.

Therefore, the diamond system phase of billiards covers a method which will allow anyone to go up to a billiard table and figure out a natural angle 3-cushion shot.

However, the principal points should be gone over again, plus a couple of factors worth knowing in advanced play:

Strike the cue ball on the direct center line, with favoring natural, running english.

Memorize the object and cue ball numbers and the starting points they cover.

Memorize the connecting diamond numbers — they are the basis of the entire system.

The inside numbers on the table are object ball (diamond) numbers which are from 1 to 7 on the two side rails (the corner is 8); and cue ball (outside) are position numbers from 1 1/2 to 5 on the side rails and at the head (lower rail) of the table are 6, 7 and 8. Connecting fourth cushion diamonds at the head of the table are object ball numbers 7, 6, 5, 4, 3 and 2; seven and five being halfway between the spots (diamonds) because the table is twice as long as it is wide.

The cue ball's starting position is second in relation to the side rail object ball numbers. A ball hit from cue ball position No. 5 to Diamond No. 4 on the opposite rail will go to Diamond No. 1 on the third rail and to Diamond No. 7 at the head of the table.

The starting point of the system is built on the fact that when the cue ball strikes the third cushion at object ball location No. 2, it will travel from this point on the third rail directly into the opposite lower corner of the table.

So the foundation of the system is mathematical. The numbers opposite the diamonds on the rails represent the way the table is numbered when you are standing at the head of the table. In calculating object ball "locations," the diamonds retain their regular numbers from 1 to 7, counting away from the first short rail which the cue ball will hit. *The low numbers always start at the opposite end of the table from where you are standing to shoot.*

In order to determine where you want the cue ball to strike the third cushion, you subtract the object ball location number from the cue ball position number; the result giving you the exact spot to hit the first cushion with the cue ball.

Employ just enough force of stroke to carry the cue ball several feet past the place where the cue ball counts on the second object ball. Practice will give you this "touch." Always remember that if you use excessive speed, it will shorten the angle of the cue ball traveling around

(Photograph No. 36)—3-Cushion Bank Shot from corner, using Diamond System calculation, shooting from cue ball position No. 5.

the table; if you employ less speed, it will lengthen the angle of the cue ball; and, in either case, you will miss the billiard.

The same method of calculation is used when the balls are located on any imaginary line between the diamonds or on any extension of the lines shown in the foregoing diagrams.

Shoot directly on a straight line "through" or "at" the diamonds on the first (side) cushion when playing from the end (short) rails; and "opposite" the diamonds on the first (side) rail when shooting from the side (long) cushions.

An advanced factor to note is that as you travel down the rail with the cue ball location, you will find that after you reach cue ball position No. 3½ and still using No. 2 as the object ball location point on the third cushion, the angle changes to some extent at this point. You will see that the point of the cue ball contact on the third cushion is a little above, instead of on — opposite — Diamond No. 2. As you move further down the rail, a more pronounced change is evident.

In contacting the third cushion, the cue ball will hit a little further above Diamond No. 2 each time the cue ball position moves a little further distance down the table.

However, continue to figure Diamond No. 2 as the third cushion contact in your subtraction and addition. Actual play will teach you the fact that you must allow this extra amount of distance above Diamond No. 2 in getting an accurate location of your object ball.

But don't bother with this technicality when first learning the system. This variation of angles starts at the half-way mark of the table from both side and end rails. In other words, you will notice this variation in angles after the cue ball position number passes Diamond No. 4 on the side rail or Diamond No. 7 on the end cushion. Lack of this knowledge is the main reason why many "system" shots are missed by the average player.

When an object ball must be hit first, use the edge of the first object ball as the location number of the cue ball. That is, you determine the point of contact on the first cushion after you hit the first object ball by the same method you determine the cue ball position for a bank shot. Simply locate the position of the object ball for your starting point, just the same as if the object ball was the cue ball. In short, in bank shots — the cue ball is the base of calculation; but when an object ball must be hit first—the object ball is the calculation base.

SPECIFIC RULES

Find line of direction from the third cushion before the count, through the count to the next or fourth cushion.

The number on the third cushion you strike is the object ball location number.

Determine the position number of your cue ball by getting the approximate direction or course of the angle your cue ball should start for the first cushion.

Subtract the object ball location number from the cue ball position number to determine which will be the diamond number you strike on the first cushion.

If the cue ball is not exactly on a cue ball number, draw an imaginary line from the nearest cue ball number to your first cushion number and then play to your first cushion along a line exactly parallel with the imaginary line.

Strike the cue ball on the center line with natural, running english.

In order to find a *natural* angle, you will have to subtract the object ball number from the cue ball number and arrive at some numerical difference for the shot to be on. Therefore, you shouldn't attempt shots that call for a greater object ball number than 4½ — as you can't subtract 5 from 5. If this occasion comes up, play the shot from the other end and other side of the table, which necessitates a four or more cushion shot.

The total of the two object ball numbers on the two long (side) rails *MUST* always equal the cue ball starting (position) number.

ROLL OF THE BALL

Test the long and short ends of the table by rolling a ball against and with the nap of the cloth. The cloth always is put on the bed of the table with the nap running to the foot. Therefore, a cue ball rolling toward the head of the table, against the nap, will sag away — "long"— from the side (long) cushion, while a ball rolling toward the foot, with the nap, will slightly curve (on many shots) toward the long (side) rail —"short"— to whichever side, of course, it happens to be rolling.

(Photograph No. 37)—Around-the-table 5-cushion bank shot, played by use of the "Diamond System", as caught by the repetitive flash camera. (By courtesy of *Life Magazine* and Photographer Gjon Mili.)

CONCLUSION

FROM NOW ON • IT'S UP TO YOU

There is little need to summarize the most important points covered in "Billiards As It Should Be Played." I have tried to explain every detail in the briefest, most vivid way. Every point covered is important, and they work together, like links in a chain. And everyone knows that a chain is no stronger than its weakest link. That is my best explanation of what you should know and do in order to become a good billiard player and gain the utmost enjoyment from this great indoor game.

You can attain these two objectives if you follow my instructions. By all means, don't underestimate the importance of fundamentals. I am certain that I cannot overemphasize the necessity of your religiously following these vital factors from A to Z.

In closing, I have put together a *"Glossary of Terms"* that I hope you will find most helpful.

So a final word —

Stand at the table firmly, well balanced on your feet. Have a good cue grip and well-made, solid bridge.

Make all strokes with the cue in a smooth, positive and confident stroke with correct speed.

Aim at the spot on the cue ball you intend to strike — and strike it there.

Aim at the point on the object ball you want to hit— and hit it there.

Concentrate on the shot at hand.

Never become discouraged when you miss. Life for most of us is a succession of "misses"— always keep *TRYING*.

Play the game like a gentleman — like a student. Be certain of yourself and your shots and you will spend many happy hours as you become better and better at this grand game.

In conclusion, I have a parting tale. It again illustrates the old query, "Why should the spirit of mortal be proud?"

Welker Cochran and I were playing a recent match in a Pacific Coast club. One of the club members was referee. I made a run of two in my first inning. The referee announced, "Two for Mr. Hope."

"The name is Hoppe," I advised him.

Welker shot and my inning came again. I missed. "Nothing for Mr. Hop," droned the referee.

"Hoppe," I again advised.

"Say," called one of the spectators to the referee, "Don't you know that man's name?"

"No," confessed the referee, and turning to me, asked, "What is it?"

"Hoppe," I told him. "Two syllables."

He got it right after that.

Forget the impractical suggestions of the average player. He may want to help you, but there is only one definite outlined method for success, and I have tried to cover this in entirety. But you must constantly practice.

Finally, stop hoping you will make billiards and wishing that you will make this and that shot. Pay strict attention to fundamentals, and the explanations of the salient points from there on. You will be pleasantly surprised to see how quickly and definitely you will be rewarded by good billiard playing that will bring to you the pleasure, personal satisfaction, and achievement you seek with the ivories on the green baize.

In short, it's up to you! As I said in the beginning, anyone can learn to play a good game of billiards — so, take both my and your cue and go to it, my billiard friend.

GLOSSARY OF BILLIARD TERMS

(Explanation of Technical Terms Employed in the Game of Billiards)

Balkline (18.1 and 18.2)—
Lines are drawn on the table 18 inches from each of the four cushions, making nine spaces. The center space is unrestricted. The other eight spaces are restricted as to number of points being made in them. In 18.1 Balkline, at least one of the object balls must be driven out of a restricted space before consecutive shot in this space is permissible; in 18.2, at least one of the object balls must be driven out on or before the second consecutive shot in any one restricted space.

Bank—
Shooting the cue ball into a cushion before striking an object ball. In pocket-billiards, it also means to drive the object ball into a cushion before pocketing it.

Bed—
The base of the table.

Best Game—
The player's low inning game of the tournament, etc. In other words, the game the player required the least number of innings to run out his string of required points.

Big Ball—
An object ball near a cushion or in a corner of the table, affording a chance to count by hitting it with the cue ball either straight on or off a cushion or cushions.

Billiard—
Generally means a "Carom" or point scored.

Break—
The opening shot — breaking the balls.

Bridge—
The player's hand that holds the tip end of the cue on the table.

Carom—
Causing the cue ball to strike both object balls on the same stroke or hitting an object ball and then going to a point on a cushion.

Carom Billiards—
The different games played under the general name of Carom Billiards are played on a table without any "openings" or pockets. The method of scoring in these games is usually by causing the cue ball to "Carom" or strike from one object ball to another, which counts one point or billiard.

Challenge Match—
Championship competition between the world's champion and the runnerup in the last world tournament; the winner recognized as world's titleholder.

Count—
A point or billiard scored; and also is often used to refer to the score as, "What's the Count?"

Cue Ball—
The ball a player shoots with or strikes with the cue.

Cueing the Ball—
Striking the cue ball with the tip of the cue.

Cushion—
The four rails around the table that the balls strike.

Cushion-Caroms—
One-cushion billiards. A point is counted when the cue ball comes in contact with the second object ball, after striking one object ball and touching one or more cushions in any order.

Dead-Ball—
Striking your cue ball absolutely dead-center. More often, striking the first object ball very full, too. Dead-ball shots must be made by also striking the first object ball at least three-quarters full.

Diamonds—
The 20 spots on the wooden rails of the table; seven on each long rail and three on each short rail; used in calculating the diamond system.

Draw—
Cueing your ball below center, causing it to reverse its original forward direction, then go more to one side, or back, from object ball or cushion it strikes.

Drive—
This term is used almost exclusively in playing on the Carom table (a table without pockets). It means to "force" or drive the object ball. It usually signifies "driving" the ball one or more cushions and causing it to return to the desired place for position on the next shot.

Duck—
Safety (see safety).

18.1 Balkline—
See "Balkline."

18.2 Balkline—
See "Balkline."

English—
The result of striking the cue ball on one side, causing it to twist, or spin. Sometimes referred to as "twist."

First (1st) Object Ball—
The first ball hit by the cue ball.

Five-Cushions—
A shot in which the cue ball strikes five cushions before making the count on the second object ball.

Follow—
Cueing your ball above center, causing it to continue its original forward course, either directly forward, or forward to the right or left, after it strikes an object ball or cushion.

Four-Cushions—
A shot in which the cue ball strikes four cushions before making the count on the second object ball.

14.1 Pockets—
The championship pocket-billiard game. Continuous with 125 points constituting a contest. Fourteen of the 15 balls are pocketed in each frame (after being

racked) with the 15th ball always remaining on the table while the other 14 pocketed balls are racked. Scoring is continued until all but one of the unpocketed balls in each frame (after being racked) have been pocketed. Each pocketed ball is scored as one point.

Foul—
An unfair stroke; striking the cue ball twice with the same stroke (sometimes called a push-shot); touching a ball with the cue without delivering a stroke; touching a ball with clothing, etc.; making a move contrary to rules of the game.

Frame—
See Inning. Also denotes when total of 14 or 15 balls have been pocketed in pocket-billiards.

Freeze—
See "Frozen."

Frozen—
Two or more balls absolutely touching each other with no space between them—or one ball lying against a cushion in the same manner.

Grip—
The player's hold on the butt of the cue.

High Grand Average—
The total average of points made per inning by the player throughout the entire tournament or number of designated games. Figured in the same manner as high single average.

High Individual Average—
The player's best game or best low inning game average, figured to the decimal point, which shows the average number of points scored per inning. Arrived at by dividing the number of innings played into total points scored.

High Run—
The largest total of consecutive points scored by a player in any single inning, or turn at the table.

High Single Average—
See High Individual Average.

Inning—
A player's turn at the table, terminated by a miss.

In Stroke—
Meaning a player is playing well with a perfect, even. rhythmic stroke of the cue.

Ivories—
The balls used in all styles of carom billiards; being made of ivory.

Jump—
When the cue ball jumps off the bed of the table. Jumping over an object ball to strike a cushion is not permissible.

Kiss—
When the cue ball comes into accidental contact with an object ball before a billiard or point has been effected. When the object balls come into contact with each other by accident, which more than often costs a point.

Lag—
Sometimes called "Bank." Players bank or "lag" for the opening shot — driving their balls to the end rail and trying to bring them back as close as possible to the head of the table rail. Closest ball to this rail is winner of the lag or bank.

Leave—
Expression denoting the position in which the balls rest after a shot is completed. Therefore, the phrases: Good or bad leave or leaves.

Long—
When a ball rolling toward the head of the table is curved very slightly *away* from the long rail because of the effect of the nap of the cloth, in technical billiard vernacular it is said to roll "long."

Masse—
Causing the cue ball to curve out and around, or go forward and then back, before counting. This is caused by elevating the butt of the cue and striking "down through" the ball from the top side.

Match Play—
Championship competition between two players.

Minnie—
Used in the billiard vernacular of the experts to define a "natural" or "very easy and hard to miss" shot.

Miscue—
An improperly delivered stroke. Usually caused by striking the cue ball too far to one side, too high, or too low, causing the cue tip to slide off the cue ball. (See diagram in "Cueing the Ball" chapter and read instructions.)

Natural—
An easy shot which only requires natural direction of the cue ball with no english, draw or follow.

Natural English—
See Running English.

Nurse—
Keeping the balls close to the cushion in straight-rail; hugging the rail.

Object Ball—
The ball hit by the cue ball.

One-Hole—
When a player has a score one point short of game point he is said to be in the one-hole.

Pocket-Billiards—
This style of billiards — and there are many variations — is played on tables equipped with four or six pockets at the corners and sides. Scoring in the different games of pocket-billiards is done by shooting or driving object balls into the pockets.

Push Shot—
A double stroke. When tip of cue still remains on cue ball as it comes in contact with the object ball.

Rack—
Place the balls correctly in the triangle for the opening shot in pocket-billiards.

Rail—
The four cushions around the table that the balls strike.

Red Ball—
One of the object balls in carom billiards. Also a style of game in which the cue ball must strike the red ball before coming in contact with the white object ball to effect a count — or billiard — or point.

Reverse English—
A spin which makes the cue ball come off a cushion at a more obtuse angle and at a slower speed than a ball hit without english. See *Running English*.

Round-Robin Tournament—
Championship competition embraces a round-robin schedule, either once or twice around. Once around is most prevalent. Round-robin means that each player plays each of his opponents.

Running English—
Slight follow and english favoring the cue ball's progress, right or left in the direction of the shot, giving the ball a natural run.

Safety—
A shot deliberately taken to try to leave the balls safe or "tough" for your opponent after they stop rolling, with no attempt or intention to make a point on the shot, is called a safety.

Scratch—
Two different definitions. In billiards it means to make a point by accident, by some turn of luck, a lucky kiss, etc. In pocket-billiards, it means a cue ball going into a pocket, which means forfeiture of one or more points.

Second (2nd) Object Ball—
The second ball hit by the cue ball.

Short—
When a ball rolling toward the foot of the table is made to curve slightly in toward the long rail by the effect of the nap of the cloth, in technical billiard vernacular it is said to roll "short."

Spots—
Marks on the table where the balls are set up for the opening shot or after a foul or scratch. Also often referred to as the marks on the rails, more commonly known as diamonds.

Spot the Balls—
To set up the balls on the right spots, as at the start of a game.

Stance—
The position of the player when addressing himself to the cue ball.

Straight-Rail—
Carom or ball-to-ball billards. A point or billiard is made by causing the cue ball to strike both the object balls on a single stroke.

String—
The number of points being played, signified by the markers used for counting on the string above the table.

Stroke—
The swinging motion of the cue in the player's hands.

System—
Refers to the 3-cushion diamond system of mathematically determining correct angles and where to strike the object balls to carom to a definite point on the cushions. (See Diamond System section, where this method is fully explained.)

Three-Cushions—
The cue ball must touch the cushions at least three times before striking the second object ball. Any order is permissible: the cue ball may strike three cushions before coming in contact with the two object balls; two cushions, object ball, another cushion or more, and then the other object ball, etc. More often the method is cue ball against object ball, then three or more cushions, and the other object ball.

Top—
Cueing the ball above center which causes a forward or "over-spin," commonly called "follow."

To the Rack—
Used to denote utter defeat of player hanging up his cue and stopping play.

Umbrella Shot—
A three-cushion shot in which the cue ball strikes two cushions before hitting the first object ball and the first cushion struck is a long rail. After the cue ball strikes the two cushions and first object ball, it then strikes the other long rail and comes off to make the count on the second object ball. (So-called because the shot seems to open up after cue ball strikes first object ball.)

REQUISITES TO REMEMBER

TO BE a good player, never forget these suggestions; billiard points (pointers) that are unwritten rules for all — beginners and advanced players — always to remember.

1. Select a cue with the proper weight, length, size of grip and general "good feel" for you.

2. Stand at the table naturally—at ease—and try to relax at all times—cultivate a good, comfortable stance.

3. Hold cue lightly in grip hand between thumb and first two fingers.

4. Hold cue at balance point, not at extreme butt end.

5. Chalk your cue at frequent intervals—see that it has sufficient chalk on tip before each shot.

6. Make a firm, bridge hand and employ a short bridge.

7. Leave your cue on the line of aim. Never allow cue to sway from side to side.

8. Follow-through the cue ball evenly and extremely on every shot regardless of whether the stroke is to impart follow, draw, center ball or english. Determine your natural stroke and stick to it. Finish your stroke at least one inch beyond where hitting cue ball.

9. Hold your cue as level as possible, except when elevation is needed, as previously explained.

10. Sight cue as you sight a gun—keep head directly over and on line of aim.

11. Strike cue ball where you aim—straight through —never permit the cue to slide off to right or left when putting english on the ball.

12. Strike cue ball at, or never more than a cue tip from, center at every opportunity.

13. Hit object ball where you aim.

14. Be natural in your every move, but employ even motion.

15. Study the fundamentals over and over again.

16. Concentrate on all fundamentals at all times.

17. Develop a certain solid style—it will come natural and when it does, stay with it.

18. Use between 18 to 20 ounce cue.

19. Use $1/2$ inch cue tips—medium, hard leather.

20. Play draw shots at every opportunity. It is the most important shot in billiards.

21. Play half-follow shots instead of thin object ball shots.

22. Make your shots the short way, if possible—that is, if two shots present themselves at one time.

23. Practice constantly and intently—with a definite object (certain shots, etc., at all times)—just a little practice will show surprising results in your play.

24. Observe the technique of expert players; not to copy any one style, but to incorporate the average desirable points of most of them.

25. Leave your cue on the line of aim.

26. Take as much effort to make the easy, natural shots as you do the hard ones. If you make the easy shots, as well as you do the tough ones, your game will improve to a much larger extent. Most players are over-confident on easy shots, and try too hard on difficult ones.

27. Strike cue ball in center, never beyond one-half to right, left, top or bottom from center to edge.

28. Avoid english to the greatest possible extent.

29. Concentrate on every shot.

30. Find your faults and correct them—one at a time.

Remember: If your position at the table is uncomfortable, it is wrong. Again study my illustrations accompanying the "Proper Position, Correct Stance" Chapter.

Find the middle, or objective point, between the two object balls, when playing a one-cushion carom, and use it as a guide.

Use the "V" course as a guide for all two-cushion caroms. Strike the cue ball below center when making a draw-shot, cue as parallel as possible to the table to prevent miscues, and use no english on any ball-to-ball draw, except to improve position.

Strike the cue ball slightly above the center (top ball) for most all three-cushion caroms. The only exception is when draw effect is needed for a sharp angle.

Leave the object balls in front of the cue ball in straight-rail, cushion caroms and balkline.

In playing the straight rail nurse, employ right english on the cue ball to get the opposite effect on the first object ball, and vice versa.

When nursing the balls on the rail, use inside, or cushion english, as little as possible, as it tends to work the balls away from the cushion.

Hit the first object ball as thin as possible in playing the masse; and the sharper the curve is to be, the more perpendicular the cue must be held.

And always remember: (1) Shoot with the right ball; (2) Chalk your cue; (3) Concentrate (don't become absent-minded, careless, indifferent or inattentive) and practice. If you do, billiard success is yours.

HELPFUL HINTS TO BEGINNERS

1. Decide how the shot should be made and stick to the decision. Shots are often missed because an alternative method is still in the mind, for instance, when the second object ball lies near a cushion and the stroke is attempted as a direct carom before the thought of making it off the cushion has been dismissed.

2. Fix the eye on the point of the ball which the cue is to strike, and address that spot. Players sometimes acquire the habit of moving the cue in some other line and shifting at the time of delivering the stroke to the spot at which they wish to strike. This obviously involves much chance of failure.

3. Don't stroke harder than is necessary to produce the desired result and bring the balls to a good position for the next shot. General hard stroking is sometimes followed by good leaves, but this is usually luck. Remember, too, that it is more difficult to strike the cue ball accurately when you use a hard stroke.

4. Chalk the cue tip before attempting any shot.

5. Keep the bridge hand perfectly rigid and hold the cue lightly in the fingers of the grip hand at the balance point. Close the forefinger loop around the cue so that it rubs in order that the cue ball may be struck without danger of the cue slipping and causing a miss or miscue.

6. Let the weight of the cue do the work, and don't forget the "Follow-Through."

7. Don't swing the cue sideways in imparting english. Keep the line of its movement parallel to the line of aim. Remember that a raised cue butt (elevation) in strokes employing english imparts a masse effect, which gives a curved path to the ball.

8. Practice the strokes which you are uncertain of; set the balls in position and play each shot again and again until you master the shot itself and the control of the positions of the balls after the shot is made.

9. Advanced masse, the art of nursing, complicated draw strokes and the Diamond System should be learned from a competent instructor.

10. Take the game seriously, study is carefully, and its value as a recreation will be greater; more fun will be forthcoming. The listless, careless player not only does not improve, but gets little out of it except a means of wasting his time. He misses the rewards in bodily and mental refreshment which earnest endeavor always brings to him.

11. There is an element of chance in billiards as in all affairs of life; but the player who depends on luck seldom improves his game. Chance is the common enemy of all players; the alibi for deficiency of execution.

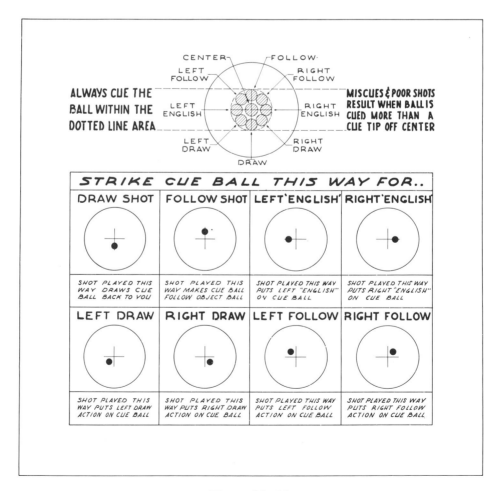

Diagram No. 96.